A User's Guide to Plone 4.3

2014 Edition

Robert Nagle

A User's Guide to Plone 4.3: 2014 Edition

Robert Nagle

Publication date December, 2014
Copyright © 2014 Enfold Systems, Inc.

Author: Robert Nagle

Editor: James Prohaska

Cover design: Clearnoodle Studio, LLC

This book is based, with permission, on the following works of gocept gmbh & co. kg, 06112 Halle (Saale), Germany; Authors Thomas Lotze, Jan Ulrich Hasecke

- *Content Management with Plone* (English and German translations, all editions)

- *A User's Guide to Plone* (English and German translations, all editions)

Table of Contents

Foreword

One of the more frequent non-technical questions I'm asked is where the name "Plone" comes from. When Alexander Limi and I met and began conceptualizing Plone-the-Software, we were also listening to a British electronic band that I had introduced to him, called Plone. The playful and minimalist sound worked well in the background as we worked, so we decided early on that 'Plone should look and feel like the band sounds.'

Plone was envisioned and designed with the end user in mind, with a simple goal: to make the day-to-day user productive in authoring and editing web pages. The Plone CMS and this book in particular, are committed to empowering everyday users with an intuitive, easy to use CMS experience. We also planned on an open source model for Plone from inception, which means that the software is free, and the source code is visible to all.

Perhaps this vision sounds utopian, but I've personally witnessed how the efforts of all kinds of people can coalesce around a single idea. Plone was created by two people who never actually met physically until a year after working on the project. That soon led to a Plone conference in my hometown of New Orleans where we launched several initiatives, including major work on accessibility and a demonstration of how Plone helps the visually impaired become more productive. In a blink of an eye, the project torch has been handed down to new developers who are continuously adding improvements and new features. The goal has always remained the same: make the daily user's job easier, and not leave any category of users behind.

This book is an extension of the Plone community. In addition to helping Plone users become more productive, it serves an important advocacy function. When a book is shared among people within an organization, it benefits the recipient as well as the purchaser. This chain of sharing has the ability to inspire others to contribute to the Plone community in new and unanticipated ways. Wouldn't it be wonderful if the next person reading this book decided to translate it into Braille or discover some way to broaden Plone's appeal? Participation is the guiding force behind the writing of this book and behind the open source movement as a whole.

Alan Runyan, Co-founder of Plone

Chapter 1. Intro to Plone

The aim of this book is to help content creators be productive with Plone, a mature content management system (CMS) with a proven track record of security, performance and extensibility. Plone is also an open source project, which means that the software is free and the source code is visible to all. Over the years, Plone has attracted users across the globe, and has generated a diverse and active community of developers who continue to create new features and add-ons.

Plone has come a long way since its creation in 1999, when three developers started the project as a front-end usability layer to the Zope Content Management Framework. Over the past fifteen years, Plone has gone through four major releases, with improvements to layout, functionality, usability and performance in every release. At the same time, the field of content management systems has progressed quite a bit—and not just for Plone. While the concepts behind most content management systems are more similar than different, each CMS implements core features differently and uses a different kind of interface. Because of Plone's approach to implementation, it is now recognized one of the most secure, and robust CMSs available, not succeptible to cross-server scripting invasions, with competitive advantages in both content management and security. There are three primary reasons why:

1. Strong Security: Plone's security model is much tighter than other CMS's, and this is one of Plone's main appeals, especially when compared with PHP-based content management systems which are succeptible to cross-server scripting attacks.

2. Dynamic Access: Plone's strong security features are linked to the dynamic access features inherent in the system. Plone can easily display a company's organizational structure, allowing private and public areas to be created within an organization. Users are designated as belonging to defined roles in order to restrict or grant access to those areas. Ordinary users, for example, lack the right to modify default styles or to make major changes to the site's layout for pages they create. Designated content creators have control mainly over the main content area, which they edit with TinyMCE, a rich-text web editor.

3. Accessibility and Standards Compliance: Plone has had a strong emphasis on standards compliance and accessibility ever since it was the first 100% XHTML and CSS-Standards compliant CMS in the world. It has remained ahead of the curve since then. As a result, Plone's appeal reaches to thousands of organizations of all sizes, and has become the preferred choice for many universities, businesses, and public agencies.

Goals for this Book

Like previous editions, this book is directed toward people who will be creating and editing content on a Plone site. Unlike previous editions, this edition of the book will cover many routine tasks performed by the user with the Site Administrator or Manager roles. Developers and system administrators should find useful insights about Plone from the user's perspective, but it should be clear that the primary goal of this book is helping the content creator to create content.

Over the years, people have customized Plone for many different situations and content areas, and as a result, Plone enjoys a vast ecosystem consisting of (mainly) open-source and proprietary add-ons. Site developers have the ability to download and install business-oriented features (such as shopping carts and classified ads), publishing features (books production, blogs & documentation development), file repositories, multimedia (embedded video players, flash support), nonprofits (wikis, discussion boards) and corporate Intranets (LDAP authentication).

Since the ecosystem is constantly growing to serve a variety of endmarket needs, it does not make sense to try to enumerate the broad range of possible features and customizations available in Plone. Instead, this book will focus on providing an in-depth understanding of the most important "out-of-the-box" features found in a generic Plone installation. Why do this?

First, any customized content types found on your company's Plone site are likely to be based upon the original content types included with Plone. Even if your company's site has a content type called *Meeting Minutes*, it will probably contain many features from the generic Page content type.

Second, while there are many add-ons and customizations available for Plone which can make it easier to use, we recommend developing an understanding of Plone's fundamentals first. Once you learn about the use of basic content types, workflows, and sharing, you will have mastered what I believe to be the "hard parts" about Plone, and will be in a far better position to understand customizations and add-on features.

Third, core features for Plone are less likely to change than features in add-ons. This means that the information in this book should remain useful even after Plone is upgraded to a newer version. While each major upgrade adds and remove features, the core functionality doesn't change that radically (except in a positive way). On the other hand, information about third-party plug-ins becomes dated pretty quickly. In older editions of Plone books I have accumulated over the years (including an earlier edition of this book), I've observed that the sections covering the generic features remain the most useful.

Terminology

Most of the chapters will assume that you are an ordinary user, with no elevated privileges. However, some sections will assume that a user has either the Manager role or Site Administrator role. Privileges and security are discussed thoroughly in Chapter 7, *Sharing* [111]. When the book refers to the "**Admin user**", it is simply shorthand for a user with either the Manager role or Site Administrator role. The chapters that cover sharing and the publication process assume that multiple users are working together with different user roles.

The book uses two more informal terms: "site developer" and "site planner." These terms are used informally here to designate the person who writes the customizing code or Theme CSS (site developer), or the person who decides site policies, deployment methods and add-on tools to use (site planner). Both the site developer and site planner have the Manager role in Plone. Many tasks which the site planner or site developer work on lie outside the scope of this book.

How this Book is Organized

This book is organized into three sections. The first section of the book discusses how the content creator creates and edits content. The second section covers the publication process and how to share things with other users and roles. The third section discusses features which only the Admin user can perform, and includes a chapter on *Site Setup* to provide a reference guide to the *Site Setup* control panel and some basic recommendations.

Please note that some advanced topics (like portlets, collections and sharing) were previously available only to users with the Manager role. However, the new Site Administrator role (introduced in Plone 4.2) can now perform many of these same functions. Generally, if both the Site Administrator and Manager have the right to configure something, it will be covered here.

Near the end of the book is a chapter about improving navigation and findability. These issues can present special challenges in Plone, and this chapter offers tips and strategies for improvement.

Also at the end are two appendices about workflows and TinyMCE, as well as a glossary.

Changes since the 2010 Edition

What's New about Plone 4.3

Since the release of Plone 4.0 in 2010, a variety of changes have been made to Plone, some easier to notice than others. Many changes relate to backend issues, or to developer tools for building better content types, themes or plugins. While many of the changes are geared toward helping Admin users, here are some things which the ordinary user might notice:

- Overall improvement in site performance. In the past, some have complained (with varying justification) that Plone sites were slow. After 4.0, lots of work has gone into making Plone faster on key benchmarks.

- Advanced Search now has fewer filtering options and an easier-to-use interface. Also, search results include links to the item's parent folder(s). For example, the listing for a single item in search results will also show something like: **Located in Academics/ Anthropology Department/ Research** where each part of the path is actually a link to that specific folder.

- A new Site Administrator role has been added. It's a step below the Manager role, but it can perform many of the functions previously only available to a user with the Manager role: managing users, editing collections, editing portlets and accessing selected Site Setup control panels.

- Small improvements have been made to the TinyMCE rich text editor to improve consistency and performance on all browsers. Previous versions had included two different rich text editors. Kupu, the older editor, has now been removed in favor of TinyMCE, which is more popular and less buggy.

- In the pop-up within the editor for inserting links, it is no longer possible to browse to find anchors of content items other than the current item you are editing.

- Several new optional buttons have been added to the TinyMCE editor. Two buttons, (*Table Row Properties* and *Cell Properties*) have been removed.

- There is now a system to moderate comments and configure RSS feeds. Again, these things generally require someone with Admin privileges.

- There is a much better interface for editing collections.

- A global setting now lets you hide all user information and modification dates for anonymous visitors. (*Site Setup --> Security*). Logged in users will still be able to see these things.

- Users with the manager role can add/edit/switch Plone themes on the fly. There is now a built-in *Theme Editor* which allows the user with the manager role to tweak the CSS.

- A new content type framework called *Dexterity*. *Site Setup* has a through-the-web (TTW) tool which allows the Site Administrator or Manager to create new content types by using existing form widgets and behaviors. The catch here is that even though Plone has this TTW tool, it is still necessary for a developer to configure programmatically a "view" which presents the content item to the visitor. For now, there is no TTW method for doing this (although that might come later).

- Better support for HTML 5 and JQuery.

What's New about the Book

Because this book has always focused on core features, the content should remain relevant for some time. Here are some additions and changes:

1. Because of the new Site Administrator role, the book now focuses more on the routine tasks which the Site Administrator or Manager users perform. (As mentioned above, the book uses the phrase "Admin user" to refer to either the Site Administrator or Manager). In the appendix, there is a table which compares which tasks can be performed by which role.

2. There is a new chapter about content rules. While content rules have been discussed in previous editions, they merit an extended treatment here, given the new role of the Site Administrator and the improvements to the Content Rules control panel.

3. There are major revisions to the Collections chapter, which describes the new interface.

4. There is a new chapter about configuring RSS feeds and comments, and recommended strategies for configuration.

5. New recommendations about how the Admin user can tweak the TinyMCE editor to make it more user-friendly.

6. Tips on how to delete content, and how users with Manager role can manage content deletions, or undo them.

About the Examples

Content management can be explained more easily with real-life examples. The examples we will use here will be Pendelton State College, a fictional university which was used as a setting for the 1990s sitcom *Third Rock from the Sun*. As you may recall, the main character was Dick Solomon, an extraterrestrial High Commander who assumes a human identity, and soon after, develops a human role as a physics professor at Pendelton. So what does this fictional, "real-life" example have to do with Plone? Well, many educational organizations prefer Plone because it is so easy to clone new sites and setup users and groups--as easily as Dick Solomon worked his way into the ranks of Pendelton!

Other Places to Find Help

First, rather than provide URLs as footnotes, I am just going to provide a generic bookmark URL which contains relevant/interesting links for readers of this book. All URLs will be listed at this URL. **http://www.enfoldsystems.com/support/a-users-guide-to-plone.html**

Plone.org has excellent documentation if you know where to find it. The **Plone 4 User Manual** on plone.org covers many of the subjects mentioned in this book (albeit in much less depth and often out-of-date). It is an excellent reference. The Plone forums also tend to be a good place to find help although you may find that the forum caters more to developers than end users.

Changes, Errata, Etc.

Even the best-edited technical books will have errors, and I will keep an ongoing list of any errors/corrections as I become aware of them. You can email them to me at (userguide@enfoldsystems.com). Check the same **http://www.enfoldsys-tems.com/support/a-users-guide-to-plone.html** to see page listing errors and corrections.

Chapter 2. Quick Guide to Creating Content

To begin creating content, we are going to first create a content item as a sample user. In this case, you will be doing so as an ordinary user named Dick Solomon.

Getting Your Bearings

Let's get your bearings in the Plone content management system. First, you will need a user name and password. Usually this will be given to you by the person managing the Plone site. To log on, choose the **Log in** option at the top right side of the Plone site. You will know you are logged in when you see your user name listed at the top right.

Common Login Issues:

- **Password doesn't work?** Perhaps the CAPS LOCK is on or you have mistyped the user name or password. Assuming that the site is correctly configured, pushing the Request Password will send an email associated with the user. The email will contain a URL that can be used to reset your password.

- **"Insufficient Privileges to view this page."** There are situations in which the Plone site will correctly log you in, but you will be unable to view a specific URL. That happens when the specific page has restricted access or has not yet been published. Usually just clicking a link to the home page will bring you to a legitimate page. In rare cases when the site is misconfigured, you may not be able to see the home page URL as well. If that is the case, the problem is not with your account but probably a sitewide problem which only an Admin user can solve.

Figure 2.1. User Name drop-down list

After logging in, your name will appear on the top right of the Plone site. Clicking on your name will reveal the "Dashboard" and "Preferences" drop-down options.

If you have successfully logged in, you can now access your Dashboard and Preferences. These are options which appear at the top right of the web page after you have logged in. Generally, it is ok to accept the default values here.

- **Dashboard** is a URL which lets you see content which specifically pertains to your user account. This could include items you have written, group portlets or other content personalized for the user or group.

- **Preferences** is also found under the drop-down menu after you log on. It will list some common fields which apply globally to your user account. That includes biographical fields.

  - **WYSIWYG Editor**. TinyMCE is the default rich text editor (see Chapter 3, *The Rich Text Editor* [21]). But here you can also choose to choose a simple HTML textarea editor instead of a WYSIWYG editor like TinyMCE.

  - **Enable External Editing**. Plone has special server tools which make it possible to edit and upload content in a third-party editor program instead of doing it through the web browser. Your site planner or developer will need to install and enable these tools for them to work. But Plone already uses an easy-to-use rich text editor, so this option is rarely needed.

  - **Allow Editing of Short Names**. Determines if Short Names (also known as IDs) are changeable when editing items. If Short Names are not displayed, they will be generated automatically. Generally it's ok not to enable this option.

Personal Information This tab on the Preferences will let you fill out personal data for other users to see. The generic version of Plone lets you add a full name, email, home page, biography and location, as well as a photo of oneself. By default, clicking on a content item's byline will bring the site visitor to the author's personal information page. Note that the Admin user has an option to hide bylines (in *Site Setup --> Security*).

Knowing Your Rights

Before you can create or edit content, your account needs the right to do so. That depends on the type of account you have, the groups you belong to, and the security settings for the Plone site or folders in that site.

The interface itself will let you know if you have the right to create or edit a certain content item. If you are logged in, certain clues will let you know where you can add content and which kinds of content you can edit.

1. **Viewing Content.** If an item has been published, it should normally be viewable. In some cases, it will not be viewable. If this happens, you will see a security message ("Insufficient Privileges to view this page)." This could happen if an older item has been removed or retracted or even moved into a different folder. (A site developer or user with the Manager role can configure the 404 error messages for malformed URLs so that it does not sound overly alarming).

2. **Adding New Content.** If your user account is able to modify a content item in the current folder, the word **Add New** will appear on the task bar above the TinyMCE editor. If you click on **Add New,** a drop-down list will reveal a number of choices about what type of item you can add. (Note: the Admin user can limit the number of different types which appear here).

Figure 2.2. The Add New drop-down menu

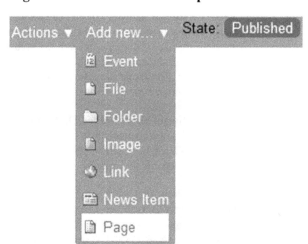

If you are able to see Add New at the right side of the toolbar, that means you have the rights to add new content to the current folder.

3. **Editing Content** If your user account is able to modify a content item, the word **Edit** will appear on the horizontal task bar right above the content.

4. **Publishing content** If you have the ability to publish the content (and to change the state of an item), there will be a drop-down option under **State**. One option underneath will be Publish (or Submit, depending on your site's default publication workflow). *Published* means that the content has already been published or that you are inside a folder which has

already been published. This is covered in greater detail in Chapter 8, *Collaborative Editing: Workflows* [129]

5. **Sharing content** If you have Edit rights to the content item, you can also assign the Add/Edit/View right to another user. That user will have edit rights for the content items you have assigned to him. Editing rights can also be granted so the user can access particular options on the content toolbar.

Your rights for adding and editing a content item may depend on the item itself as well as its location on the web site. (Sharing and restricting access to content will be covered in depth in Chapter 7, *Sharing* [111]).

Content Toolbar

When creating or editing content, you will be using features on the content toolbar which shows the available options. Most of the time, you will not see all of these options but only the options you have the permission to use. The inverted triangles to the right of options indicate that pressing it will reveal additional options in a drop-down menu.

Figure 2.3. Content Toolbar (for a Folder)

Here is a brief description of what each option means:

- **Contents** (visible in folders only). Clicking this will show the items contained in the folder and permit you to perform actions on multiple items.

- **View**. When this tab is selected, it shows how the content item as it generally appears to the anonymous visitor.

- **Edit**. When this is selected, you can edit fields and create content using the rich text editor.

- **Sharing.** This allows you to view who has permissions to this content item and bestow permissions to other users.

- **Actions**. This drop-down list will allow you to perform actions which affect the current content item. This includes Cut, Paste, Copy, Check Out, Check In. For example, if you choose Cut, the entire item will be cut and put into memory, so that when you go into another folder where you have permissions to do so, you can Paste it there.

- **Display** (visible in folders only). This offers various styles for displaying items in a folder.

- **Add New**. (visible in folders only) This drop-down will list all available item types which you can add here.

- **State** (Published). The State has a drop-down menu will shows your options for which state to put the current item into. Besides the word State, the current state of the item is shown. (Here, the items' state is *Published*).

There is one additional option in the content bar which is not shown:

- **Rules** appears to users with the Site Administrator account and allows them to activate a content rule about the current content item. It is generally not relevant to content creators.

If none of the options are listed (and the content bar itself is not visible), that means you don't have any permissions for the current content item.

Adding & Editing Content

For the rest of this chapter, we will now assume that you have the ability to add and edit content. **Important Note:** The URLs used here are simply examples to illustrate Plone's functionality, and you should follow the provided screenshots rather than going to the example URLs, which are inactive. The processes described in the examples will guide you as you follow along on your own Plone site.

For this example, the user will be "Dick Solomon," a fictional physics professor at a fictional university. As a professor, he has a Plone folder specifically for content created by him.

1. Navigate to your Plone page where content can be added, either by typing in the URL or navigating to the appropriate folder from the contents on the Home page. In this example, Dick Solomon would go to the URL for a Plone folder where content can be added: **http://plone4.clients.enfold-systems.com/academics/physics-department/faculty-pages/dick-so-lomon/**

2. On the top right tab, there will be a menu item **Add New**. If you click on that region of the menu bar, a list of options will be revealed, indicating all the content types which Dick Solomon can add. (See diagram.) In this case, the available options are Event, File, Folder, Image, Link, News Item, Page. Choose the **Page** option. (Each content type will be covered in greater detail in Chapter 4: *"Item Types "* (page 56)).

3. Add Title. After you click **Page** , you will see an **Edit** Screen consisting of several fields and a series of tabs. Your cursor will be on the **Title** field, so if you click anywhere else before typing a title, Plone will show an error. (In fact, Title is the only field which is required when creating a page). For this example, write "Home Page for Dick Solomon."

4. Add Summary. Next, you will type a description in the **Summary** field. This is an optional field, but it is helpful in two ways. First, the summary will appear in search results and also in partial views, like Collections. Second, this summary will also appear in the description. If you choose the View Source option in your browser (usually a right-click option in most browsers), you will see this line of code at the top of the HTML:

```
<meta   content="Home   Page   for   Dick   Solomon."
name="description" />
```

5. At this point, you can start typing in the Body Text section. If you want, you can click on the Toggle Full Screen mode (the icon on the far of the rich text editor) to have the Body Text area cover the entire web browser.

Figure 2.4. Editing Screen for a page

You must enter a value for title.

- **Make a hyperlink.** After typing in a sample paragraph, it is time to make a hyperlink. To do this, use your mouse to highlight one or more words.

Figure 2.5. Inserting a Link

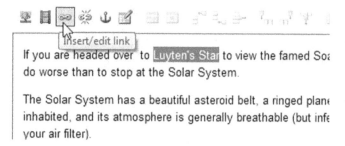

You must highlight the text for your link before the Insert Link button will be available.

Click the icon in the rich text editor that says Insert/Edit Link. (If it is grayed out, you haven't highlighted any word(s) in the body of your text). The Insert/Edit pop-up screen will appear. From the top, choose **External**.

Figure 2.6. Inserting an External Link

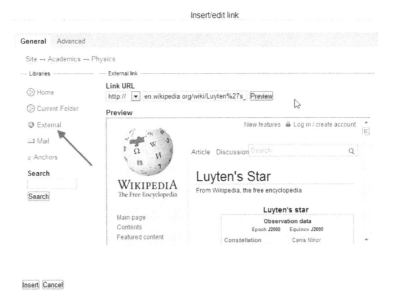

To add a traditional URL as a hyperlink, first click External on the left column.

After you choose External, the pop-up window will change to reveal a field for External Link. You will paste or type the URL into this field.

If you need to change this URL, you would simply click the same Link icon again. To remove the hyperlink, you would click on the link in your text and click on the Remove Hyperlink button.

• **Adding an image.** You can also add an image from your computer directly to the page you are editing. To do this, click on the image icon on the rich text editor. A pop-up screen will ask you whether you want to insert an image which has already been uploaded or whether you wish to upload a new image. In this case, you will wish to upload your own graphic, so click on the button that says **Upload** file.

Figure 2.7. Uploading an Image

After you click the Insert/Edit image button, the option to upload an image will appear.

After you do this, extra fields will be visible at the bottom of the **Add Image** pop-up screen.

Figure 2.8. Selecting Image options

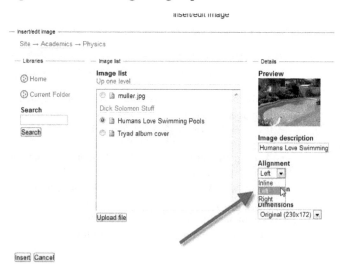

Choose left/right in the alignment field if you wish have the image on the left or right side of the page (with text wrapping around it).

Choose **Choose File** and navigate to where the image is on your computer. *Note:* There are two additional fields to fill out about the image. **Title** is whatever name for give to it (it can be multiple words and will appear as alt-text when the mouse hovers over the image) and **Image Description** is a text account of the image. Additionally, several other options will open up.

- **Alignment**. Choose left to make the image flush left against the page with text wrapping around it. Inline means that the image will occupy its own block and force the text to continue below it.

- **Link Title**. It generally is a good idea to give your links captions.

- **Dimensions**. This offers you a variety of sizes that the image can appear in. Ideally you should use the original size whenever possible.

At this point you can click **OK** and the image will appear in the main body of text.

- Before we save, let us enter a **Change Note**. This will provide useful information if we need to revert to a previous save.

Figure 2.9. Typing a Change Note

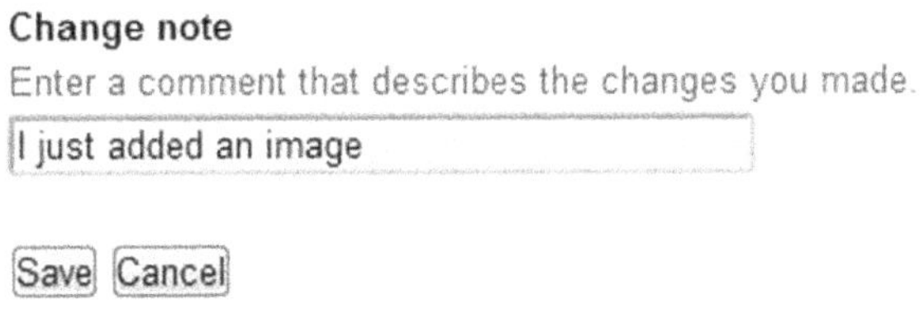

Change note

Enter a comment that describes the changes you made.

I just added an image

Save Cancel

Change Notes make it easy to identify a particular version of a content item on the History of an item.

- Now click **Save** to save the item.

Editing Metadata

Now let's return to the same item and edit some of its options.

Click the Edit tab once again. On the bar underneath the title, select **Categorization**. With the mouse you can click one or more existing tags you wish to use for this current item or enter new ones in the field provided.

Figure 2.10. Choosing a tag for your content

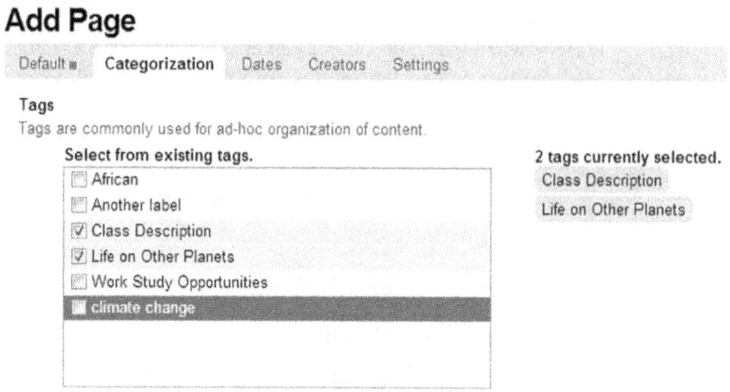

Add Page

Default ■ **Categorization**   Dates   Creators   Settings

Tags

Tags are commonly used for ad-hoc organization of content.

Select from existing tags.

- African
- Another label
- ☑ Class Description
- ☑ Life on Other Planets
- Work Study Opportunities
- ■ climate change

2 tags currently selected.

Class Description

Life on Other Planets

The user can select one or more tags to categorize the content item.

Next, enable the ability for users to make comments about this page. Click the **Settings** tab and check the option to **Allow Comments**. Also, add a remark in the Change Note for this tab and press **Save**.

Figure 2.11. Allowing Comments from Users

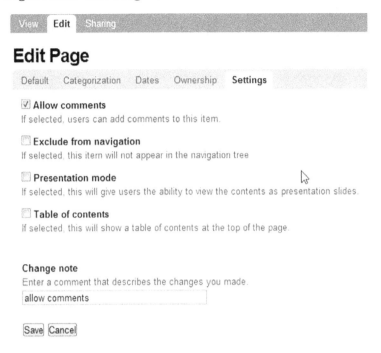

By default, comments are turned off.

Getting it Published

After you have saved, click back to the Default tab again where you will see the rich text editor again. You will notice a history hyperlink on the byline.

Figure 2.12. The History tab

After you have edited an item more than once, the history link will appear.

If you click the **History** link, a pop-up will appear showing the most recent versions (and Change Notes) and give you the option to revert to an older version. In this case, just click the black X on the top left side of the pop-up to close it.

Figure 2.13. History Popup

The History pop-up lets you compare the latest version with older versions or even to revert to a previous version.

The next step you take depends on the publication sequence for the content item on your site. Generally, you should go to the State drop-down on the top right bar. You have two primary options: **Submit for publication** and **Advanced**. (Policy is an option which works mainly for Site Administrators and is not relevant here).

Figure 2.14. Submitting for Publication

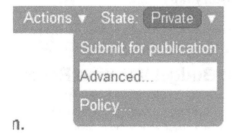

The options "Submit for Publication" or "Advanced" will let you bring the item to the next publication stage.

Submit for Publication and **Advanced** do essentially the same thing; Advanced just lets you attach a note and tentatively schedule a publication date.

Figure 2.15. Advanced pop-up dialog

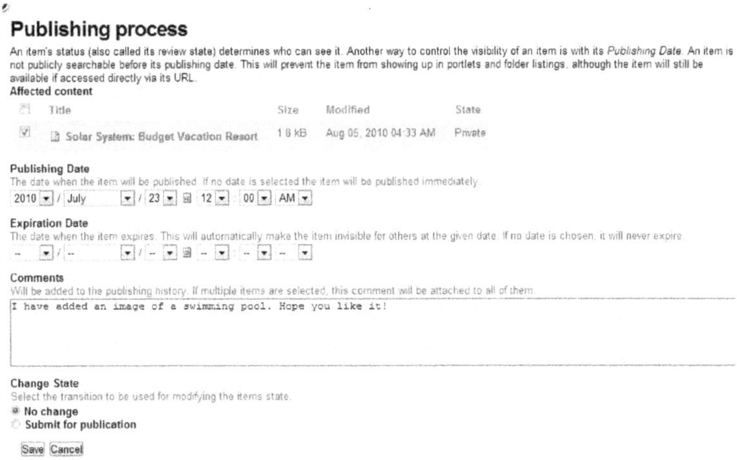

Publishing process

An item's status (also called its review state) determines who can see it. Another way to control the visibility of an item is with its *Publishing Date*. An item is not publicly searchable before its publishing date. This will prevent the item from showing up in portlets and folder listings, although the item will still be available if accessed directly via its URL.

Affected content

	Title	Size	Modified	State
☑	Solar System: Budget Vacation Resort	1.8 kB	Aug 05, 2010 04:33 AM	Private

Publishing Date
The date when the item will be published. If no date is selected the item will be published immediately.

`2010 ▼ / July ▼ / 23 ▼  12 ▼ : 00 ▼ AM ▼`

Expiration Date
The date when the item expires. This will automatically make the item invisible for others at the given date. If no date is chosen, it will never expire.

`-- ▼ / -- ▼ / -- ▼  -- ▼ : -- ▼ -- ▼`

Comments
Will be added to the publishing history. If multiple items are selected, this comment will be attached to all of them.

```
I have added an image of a swimming pool. Hope you like it!
```

Change State
Select the transition to be used for modifying the items state.
◉ No change
○ Submit for publication

`Save  Cancel`

Choosing Advanced under State lets you submit for publication, add a note and schedule a publication date.

After you press Save, the item will usually go into a Pending state. That means that someone with the Reviewer role needs to approve it for publication. This will be covered in greater detail in the chapter Chapter 8, *Collaborative Editing: Workflows* [129]. For more on the typical workflows found in Plone, see Appendix A, *Basic Plone Workflows* [223].

Alternatively, your site may allow content creators to publish directly without needing to submit it for review. If this is the case, you will have an extra option **Publish** available to you.

This is a simplified example of a single user creating a simple page using Plone. It covers about 80% of typical use for a single user. The rest of the book will go into greater detail about editor options and the publication process.

Chapter 3. The Rich Text Editor

As a content creator, you can choose to use a rich-text editor, or a simple web form for adding content. Using a rich-text editor in a CMS can save a lot of time and simplify the task of creating content, but this option also adds its own layer of complexity that can be challenging to new users.

Using an editor that is web-based presents a number of advantages for the content creator versus traditional desktop editors, most notably the improved accessibility and ease of online collaboration. Plone uses TinyMCE, a web-based rich-text editor found in several content management systems. By default, TinyMCE can handle most situations for content creators.

TinyMCE simulates the feel of "What You See is What You Get" (WYSIWYG) environments like Microsoft Word, while still allowing you to switch to an HTML code view. And because it's web-based, all the content creator needs is an internet connection to work in TinyMCE. Sounds ideal, right?

The truth is, using any rich-text editor in a web application can be tricky, especially if you don't normally work with raw HTML code. Think about just one obvious scenario: what happens if your internet connection is lost when you press the Submit button? What if your browser crashes? What steps can you take to minimize losses from these (admittedly) rare occurrences?

Whether your editor is web-based or not, many things can potentially go wrong with using a rich-text editor. In this chapter, we will cover how to perform most common tasks and how to avoid problems.

Overview of the WYSIWYG Icons

The TinyMCE toolbar includes several buttons which resemble the Microsoft Word toolbar (or the toolbar on webmail or other web-based editors). The exact appearance of the toolbar may vary depending on its specific configuration. See: the section called "TinyMCE " [209] for information about some of these configuration options. Generally though, you should find these options on your toolbar.

Figure 3.1. TinyMCE Toolbar buttons

TinyMCE toolbar buttons resemble common formatting buttons on MS Office and web-based editors.

Note: There are additional toolbar icons which the Admin user can choose to make visible on the TinyMCE toolbar. *See the section called "Additional TinyMCE Toolbar Buttons" [210].*

Right Click Menu Items

When you right-click anywhere inside the TinyMCE edit screen, some Plone-specific options will appear (See illustration below). These right-click options merely duplicate the functions already found on the editor icon bar. **Note that the paste operation in this context menu will not work;** the security settings on most browsers forbid a right-click menu from performing this kind of operation. This is normal. Instead of right-clicking, you can still use keyboard shortcuts to perform the same operations (Control-X to cut, Control-C to copy, Control-V to paste).

Figure 3.2. Right-click options from inside TinyMCE editor

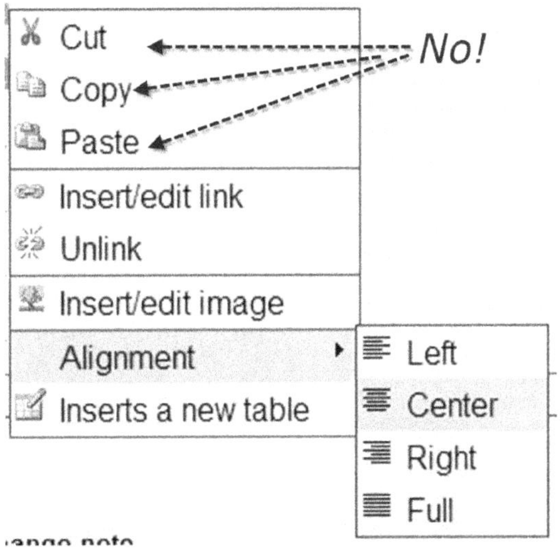

Security settings on most browsers forbid using TinyMCE's right-click paste options. The other functions still work.

Style Drop-down Box

On the TinyMCE toolbar you will notice a drop-down box with a list of styles. This drop-down box can contain default styles, or styles which are unique to your site. **The Admin user has the ability to add new styles to this drop-down box.**

Using the style drop-down is highly recommended because it lets you standardize the formatting for features specific to your organization. In the illustration below, *coursetitle* and *coursedescription* were two styles created specifically by the Admin user for this site.

Figure 3.3. Dropdown Styles in TinyMCE Editor

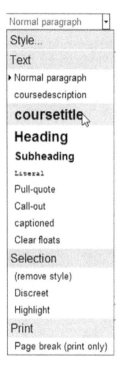

In the example above, "coursetitle" and "coursedescription" are 2 custom drop-down styles available for this site. The other drop-down options are default options in TinyMCE.

How to apply the styles listed in the style drop-down box will be covered in the section called "Using Styles " [34].

An Admin user can declare new custom drop-down styles by going to *Site Settings* --> *TinyMCE Visual Editor* and adding it to the *Styles* field. But it is still necessary for a user with the manager role to modify the theme's CSS, either by editing the css file by hand or doing it within the *Theme Editor* in *Site Setup*.

The Basics

Two special buttons on the toolbar control how the browser displays TinyMCE.

Switching from WYSIWYG mode to HTML view

The **HTML** button lets you view raw HTML code in a pop-up window, which can be helpful in trying to troubleshoot HTML issues. It can also be useful if you need to copy the raw code into another editor. If you check the **Word Wrap** box, that will automatically display HTML code so that it fits inside the HTML Source Editor window. Some code editors can produce HTML code on a single line. (In HTML, carriage returns don't generally affect the way it is displayed in the browser). Unless you are dealing with preformatted text or code excerpts, you should leave Word Wrap checked when you are editing in HTML mode.

Switching from Full Screen Mode to Regular Mode

If you plan to spend a lot of time editing a page, you should probably switch to Full Screen mode in your web browser. That gives you more room on the screen to view your content when editing.

TinyMCE has an opaque square icon which lets you switch to Full Screen Mode. Keep in mind that **you cannot save your Page when in fullscreen mode.** Before you can save, you need to click on the Full Screen mode icon to toggle back into regular mode. Note that the Admin user has the power to enable an optional Save button to the toolbar from the *TinyMCE Visual Editor* control panel in *Site Setup*.

Handling Quirky Browser Issues

Where did the Submit Button Go?

Sometimes the Submit button is hidden from you in your browser. This can happen when you are in full screen mode, which temporarily hides the rest of the Plone site while editing. To solve this problem, click on the toolbar icon **Toggle Full Screen Mode**. It is *not* necessary to click the back button on your browser; in fact, doing so will delete any edits you were working on.

Admins have the option to enable the **Save** button on the toolbar which appears even in full screen mode. This is a helpful feature and generally recommended. (To do this as the Admin user, go to **Site Setup --> TinyMCE Settings**.

Why don't the Editor icons show up in my browser?

Sometimes there is a pause between the time you start editing and the time the TinyMCE toolbar appears. Usually this happens because of latency in your computer browser or your Internet connection or the site itself. You can troubleshoot this by verifying the Internet connection and reducing the CPU/memory load on your computer (usually by closing all your browser windows and starting over).

Occasionally, the issue can arise when the Plone server is overloaded or is misconfigured. If it's taking a long time to log in to the Plone site, or if you are having trouble reading pages without being logged in, you should check with the site owners.

Playing it safe ....

As good as TinyMCE is, a thousand things can go wrong. The problem doesn't have to be with the software itself. Weird text input or browser quirkiness can account for a lot of problems. Sometimes it just helps to backtrack your steps a bit.

Undo Command

Most browsers have a keystroke that will allow you to undo the previous mouse gesture you made and to redo it if necessary.

- Control Z: undo

- Control Y: redo

In fact, if you press Control-Z multiple times, that will cause more than one change to be undone. If you press Control-Y, then the last command you undid will again take effect.

What does the browser undo when you press Control-Z? A little experimenting suggests that pressing Control-Z once will undo a mouse gesture (such as clicking on an icon or moving the cursor). It will also undo any text you typed all the way until the most recent carriage return. So if you type 5 consecutive sentences (8 lines of text total) and then press Enter, when you do the Undo Command once, all 5 sentences will be deleted.

Note: when you press the Save button, the browser wipes away a memory of all your edits and you begin again. Generally, the undo command works best when undoing only 2 or 3 times. Any more than that, and you might be better off saving the document at important spots and using Plone's versioning capability to compare different edits (See the section called "Reverting to Previous Saves (History)" [104].)

Copying unsaved work to the desktop before pressing the save button.

Unfortunately, Plone does not have a way to autosave your work inside the content management system. That means two possible dangers: your browser might crash, and your network connection might fail when you hit the Submit button. Let's discuss each situation more carefully and how to avoid losing your work.

If there is a network connection issue, all is not lost. Usually, just hitting the back button will show your unsaved content, giving you another chance to safeguard your work. Sometimes during browser crashes, the browser will reopen to the same pages and even show the input on the text fields.

TinyMCE has an optional Save button which the Admin user can enable for the entire site. I recommend this because it lets you save repeatedly without changing the view tab from Edit to View. (This and other options appear for Admin users in *Site Setup --> TinyMCE Visual Editor --> Toolbar*. For a more complete description of these optional buttons, see the section called "Additional TinyMCE Toolbar Buttons" [210].

The Precautionary Save

When relying on a web browser to create content, many people will save a copy of the content in a local text editor first before pressing the Save/Submit button in the web browser. Doing this will protect you against the possibility of your edits not being saved or the unexpected crashing of a browser.

When saving into another editor outside Plone for safekeeping, you can save content in two different ways:

1. **rendered**. This refers to content copied directly from the rich text editor when in WYSIWYG view.

2. **unrendered**. This refers to content copied from the HTML code view (i.e., by pressing the HTML icon on the rich text editor icon panel).

You can use Windows Notepad editor which comes preinstalled with every version of Windows. Or you can download a free text editor such as Note Tab Light.

There are two kinds of desktop editors you can save to:

1. a WYSIWYG word processor. (Microsoft Word, Open Office)

2. a simple text editor (Notepad, Notetab Light, any code editor)

If you paste **rendered** content into a **WYSIWYG word processor**, then many presentational elements will be saved along with the content. That includes bold, italics, indents, hyperlinks, lists and sometimes even images.

If you paste **unrendered** content into a **WYSIWYG word processor**, then presentational elements will *not* be saved along with the content. Instead raw code will appear in original form.

If you paste **rendered** content into a **simple text editor**, the simple text editor will generally ignore all presentational elements and copy only the text content itself.

If you paste **unrendered** content into a **simple text editor**, the simple text editor will show all of the code. Presentational elements will appear as raw code. (A simple text editor may have a way to display unrendered content as HTML, but here we are talking about pasting it into the code/unrendered view in the text editor).

In general, when you are making a precautionary save onto another editor, you should save the unrendered text (i.e. which becomes visible by pressing the HTML icon on the icon list of your rich text editor) and paste it into a simple text editor.

In certain cases you may wish to abandon your formatting. Perhaps you have seriously messed up your formatting and cannot correct it from the rich text editor. In this case, you can copy/paste your rendered text into a simple text editor. Doing that will transfer only the text content and allow you to start over.

Reverting to a Previous Version

Another possibility is reverting to a previous version. See the section called "Reverting to Previous Saves (History)" [104]. This makes particular sense if you messed up the template or don't exactly remember what changes you made. You can use another browser window to show the last saved version of the content item. That can help you decide whether reverting to an older saved version is advisable or whether you should just find a way to transfer manually your current edits into a previously saved version of the page.

Tips for pasting Content into a Plone page

Pasting content from one place to a Plone page can be tricky. Plone tries to figure out the best way to paste your clipboard content, but at times the result of the paste action is not always what you expect. Here are problems you may see:

- sometimes a paste will copy extra html content

- unwanted hyperlinks

- unwanted table information will be copied over

- unwanted indents for the first line of paragraphs

- list numbering is off

- extra spaces between lines

- unwanted line breaks

- carriage returns instead of new paragraphs (or vice versa)

- difficulty moving from a list to a paragraph

- discrepancy between WYSIWYG view and code view

- inability to clear styles or to apply a Plone style to pasted content

- pasted content also alters the style & formatting of existing content

- WYSIWYG mode is different from the actual presentation of the page

There are several issues involved here:

1. **Where are you copying from?** Each application handles the copy-paste operation differently.

2. **What kinds of content are you copying?** When you copy over rendered content, you may not be aware that you are copying tables and graphics and extra styles.

3. **What settings does your Plone site have for TinyMCE and HTML filtering?** Every site does HTML filtering, which means it removes certain HTML tags that could be potentially dangerous. Your site administrator may allow certain kinds of HTML code and filter others.

4. **What is the position of your cursor in the edit form when you paste content?** Sometimes styles in your pasted code will override the site's styles or any style you may have designated for a block of content in your current page.

Things to Try

Here are some general ways to deal with pasting problems.

1. If the Admin user has enabled these buttons to appear on the editor toolbar, try to paste content using the **Paste as Plain Text** or **Paste from Word** buttons. (These options appear for Admin users in *Site Setup --> TinyMCE Visual Editor --> Toolbar*). For a more complete description of these optional buttons, see the section called "Additional TinyMCE Toolbar Buttons" [210].

2. **Use the Remove Formatting feature on the TinyMCE Editor toolbar.** The Remove Formatting function is an optional toolbar button which the Admin user can enable. It is particularly good at removing font styles that affect more than one line. For example, if several paragraphs in the original source are bold-faced (with a <b> tag), pressing the **Remove Formatting** icon will remove all the bold tags for the entire portion of the text you have highlighted.

3. **Switch to HTML view and delete unnecessary tags.** This can be tedious and even a little scary for people not used to dealing with HTML code. The main problem here is that empty tags might still be present in the HTML even though you can't see them. For example, you might see something like this:

```
<ol> </ol><ol> </ol><ol><ol> </ol></ol><ol> </ol>
```

Often you can delete this kind of code in the WYSIWYG view simply by using the backspace button to remove unnecessary spaces. On other occasions, removing this code requires doing it in HTML mode.

Note: Some content management systems let you paste text with minimal formatting (*e.g.*, <a> and <b> tags) and automatically surround blocks of text with paragraph tags. Plone does not *do* this. Either you paste your content into TinyMCE without any HTML code or you paste *all* of your content as HTML code. Plone does support various markup languages (see the section called "Markup " [205]),but these work only if you have turned **off** the WYSIWYG editor from your preferences panel and if an Admin user has checked a particular markup language as an alternative format on the **Markup Settings** configuration menu in *Site Setup*.

4. **Use the backspace bar to delete unnecessary content in TinyMCE.** Manually fixing the formatting errors in TinyMCE may be tedious, but can be the best approach if you have only a few lines to correct. Probably the most common problem with a paste operation is the addition of extra line breaks. If you are dealing with four or five lines or two paragraphs, it might be more easier just to remove the line breaks with your backspace/delete button.

5. **Copy the content first into a simple text editor and then paste it into TinyMCE.** This ensures that when you paste it into TinyMCE that there will be no unnecessary HTML code. On the other hand, if the original content had a line of line breaks, this will probably not solve the problem.

6. **Check to make sure that your selected text is not mixing paragraphs with lists.** If there are extra list tags (i.e., <ol>, <ul>, <li>, <dl>) in the HTML, that may cause the WYSIWYG view to appear as though it contains extra line breaks which can't be easily removed.

7. **Create the content again from scratch in TinyMCE.** My general rule of thumb is not to spend more than 5 minutes trying to resolve a TinyMCE formatting issue; if it takes longer, it might be better just to start from scratch. If you prefer, you can refer to older versioned copies of the content item for reference or save it to another version. You can keep this older version available in a separate browser window while you try to start over on the content item.

Which text editor to use?

Almost every computer includes an editor for simple editing. Every Windows machine comes with a copy of Notepad. To open it go to *Start -->* *All Programs --> Accessories --> Notetab*. It is perfectly suited for converting pasted content into simple text or for storing your edits temporarily before you hit the Submit button.

One free Windows-based text editor that I particularly recommend is **NoteTab Light**. Here are some helpful NoteTab Light features:

- **Joining Lines** (Modify --> Lines --> Join). Sometimes when pasting content into TinyMCE, Plone will incorrectly treat each individual line as a paragraph block or add a line break <br> after individual lines. This happens because the source document contains extra line breaks, or perhaps the line breaks were made manually. Either way, fixing this problem in TinyMCE can be tedious. A better way to solve this problem is to paste the content first into NoteTab Light, select a group of lines you want to be a single paragraph and then select **Join Lines**. The editor will eliminate all line breaks except the one at the last line you selected.

- **Modify Text Case**. Modify --> Text Case --> (Choose the appropriate option). Sometimes your original text will be in all caps or all lower case, and it may be necessary to change this for more than one paragraph.

- **Global Search and Replace**. If there's a recurring line style which you wish to remove, you could simply remove all instances of the start tag and finish tag in two steps. You could also do a search for all line break tags or non-breaking spaces and replace them with nothing.

Other text editors can perform similar tasks. For example **Notepad++** is a popular Windows-editor. **Gedit** works well on Linux. **Sublime Text** has a cross-platform freeware version for Mac, Windows and Linux.

Pasting from Microsoft Word

Microsoft Word tends to produce lots of excess formatting code even if the person using MS Word hasn't done any special formatting. In the past, pasting from MS Word was very messy, but pasting from MS Word has improved a lot in Plone 4x. Try to use the **Paste from Word** function on the TinyMCE Editor toolbar. If you don't see it, that is because the site planner (i.e., the Admin user) hasn't enabled it. I recommend that this optional button be enabled for **all** Plone sites.

If your Plone site does not have access to this button, here are some tips for pasting things from MS Word:

1. Avoid pasting table of contents or columns or graphics from MS Word. They generally don't paste.

2. Don't expect lists from MS Word to paste very smoothly (especially if the list contains more than one level).

3. You may find that content pasted from MS Word contains a lot of line breaks, so you may need to remove them manually.

4. Simple MS Word tables do paste, but the table and rows won't have borders unless the style is configured as such.

5. Bold and Italic text paste ok into Plone, but colored and customized fonts and font size won't copy over. (You may see them appear temporarily in TinyMCE, but after you save, they will probably appear as simple text).

If all else fails, several online tools exist which can clean up pastes from MS Word. Just google "MS Word strip HTML" or "Convert MS Word to HTML."

Pasting from the Web Browser

Pasting from a web browser is both easy and hard. Because the browser clipboard is copying/pasting actual html code, the process of transferring content is a lot more direct; Plone merely needs to filter out any html code which the Admin user wants to filter out. This may include for example <object> and <script>.

Things to watch out for:

1. Autogenerated HTML code often includes line-by-line styling and font information. If you paste such content, Plone may not be able to filter it correctly.

2. If the <p> tag on the web page you are pasting from had an attribute special to that site (such as **<p class="article_main_text">**, Plone will not normally filter this class attribute out. In most cases, having an extra class attribute will not cause problems unless Plone has a CSS class with the same name.

3. Basic styling and font declarations may have pasted over, and these may override the Plone site's styles. (Indeed, that is how cascading style sheets work).

4. Inadvertent pasting of table information. Older HTML pages made heavy use of tables that were used mainly to help with layout. Sometimes, for example, a table may be embedded inside an article, and there is no way to avoid pasting the third-party article without also posting the table.

5. Images appear to be pasted into TinyMCE. The image isn't actually being pasted, but TinyMCE is simply rendering the image reference using the URL of the third-party image. Linking to external images on the Plone site is generally bad practice except in certain cases. You should try to use an image uploaded directly to the Plone site. If all you need from the third party website is to paste text, you should just copy the text into a simple text editor (in unrendered mode) and paste it into TinyMCE in the WYSIWYG mode.

The Admin user has the ability to strip certain kinds of HTML tags and even to enable or filter certain HTML classes. For more information, see the section called "HTML Filtering " [204] .

Pasting from a PDF Document

Pasting content from a PDF document can be the least predictable. The good news is that pasting is still possible, but it is necessary in most cases to paste the content first into a simple text editor before pasting it into TinyMCE.

Things to watch out for:

1. It may be next to impossible to copy content that overflows onto more than one page.

2. There will often be line breaks after individual lines of text in the same paragraph.

3. Columns and tables may cause TinyMCE to treat every printed line as a new paragraph (as though each line had a line break).

4. Copying from the PDF may inadvertently copy text from the headers and footers.

Unless the PDF is formatted very simply, most of the time you should copy the text you want into a simple text editor before pasting into TinyMCE. After you do so, the problem will immediately be apparent. Groups of line are not pasted as paragraphs but as individual lines. You need a way to combine the lines so that they no longer break at the same places they did in the original PDF document.

Some text editors like NoteTab Lite have a **Join Lines** function which let you do precisely this. Select the lines you wish to join, press **Control -J** and suddenly all the unwanted line breaks will disappear. If copying multiple paragraphs, you will need to run this Join Line command in NoteTab Lite on each individual paragraph. If you Select All, the text editor will run all the lines together as though the whole document were a single paragraph. That is probably not what you want.

Using Styles

There are two ways you can apply a style to a block of text: clicking on one of the toolbar buttons, or applying a style from the drop-down list.

Using one of the toolbar styles is fairly easy. Just highlight the text you wish to style and scroll to the button on the toolbar you wish to apply. If you have high-lighted more than one paragraph, when you apply the style, it will be applied to every single paragraph or div tag. (If you view the HTML code, you will see that each of the highlighted paragraphs will have a class specific to that style.

You may see something like this:

```
<p style="text-align: center; ">The rain in Spain ...
</p>
```

CSS Styles and Plone

HTML uses a language called Cascading Style Sheets (CSS) to define how content is presented on a page. When a Plone site is tailored for an organization's needs, the site developer will spend a lot of effort on a usable and attractive layout. They experiment with font sizes and families, spacing, image layout and line width.

The content creator ordinarily will not need to deal with CSS. In fact, Plone tries to give content creators only a limited ability to control the layout or look of indi-vidual pages. For content creators this is both a blessing and a curse. From the administrator's point of view, this control ensures a consistent look and feel for the entire website.

The TinyMCE Editor has a toolbar button to let you choose one of the "approved" site styles.

In some cases, when you apply a style by clicking a button on the Edit toolbar, you are adding an element to the HTML around the content. In some cases, you are simply adding or changing the class of an existing HTML tag (usually p, span, or div).

In addition to the familiar style and element buttons on the *Edit* toolbar, TinyMCE has a drop-down style list. It is relatively easy for the Admin user to add a new custom style to this drop-down list. (The Admin user can do this from *Site Setup* control panel). This is helpful if your organization has a recurring need for a nonstandard style.

Many different Edit toolbar buttons are available in TinyMCE, but not enabled by default. This includes style buttons which are rarely used (but may offer important functionality to your users). For suggestions about TinyMCE options to tweak, see the section called "Additional TinyMCE Toolbar Buttons" [210].

It is theoretically possible for the content creator to create an inline style directly in the HTML code view (by using the style attribute on the element). However, for this to work, the Admin user will need to add another Permitted style on the HTML Filter settings in *Site Setup*. (See the section called "HTML Filtering " [204]).

The Dropdown Styles

You also have the option to apply one of the styles from the drop-down list. To apply these styles, highlight the region you wish to style and select the style you want.

Hints for Using Dropdown Styles

1. If you need to undo a previous action, try pressing **Control-Z** first (the universal Undo command in browsers). This is generally more effective than choosing **(remove style)**.

2. Use the **Heading** and **Subheading** style often to break up your pages. They improve readability and (if Table of Contents is enabled), they will be converted into anchors.

3. After you have applied a drop-down style, try not to change the cursor position until you have settled on a style. It can cause confusion and even errors if you apply the new style over a different area than the region you applied the original drop-down style for.

4. If the styles for one or more paragraphs are messed up and you can't undo it, it may be easier to edit the HTML and start over.

5. It is generally not possible to apply more than one drop-down style on a selection of text.

6. **Clear Floats** is a CSS declaration that forces an element to move below another floated element. Floats are used most often when you insert images and specify that they should float left or right (to the accompanying text). When you mark something with "Clear Floats," you are specifying that all text or elements underneath this point will line break after the previous element. You could google for additional explanations and tutorials about clearing floats. Check out this URL for a great explanation of clearing floats. **http://css-tricks.com/all-about-floats/**

7. List styles don't appear in the drop-down menu unless your selection has already been made into a list (by the TinyMCE button). The same is true for table styles.

8. If a drop-down style has not been successfully applied, select a smaller amount of text (say one paragraph or even one line) and try again.

Adding custom Styles to the Dropdown list

One cool thing about Plone's TinyMCE is that it's relatively easy for an Admin user to add additional styles to appear in the drop-down list. This can be especially useful for inline styles of texts within a paragraph (such as making text a red color or a different font size or type). See the section called the section called "TinyMCE " [209].

Benefits of Starting from Scratch

As mentioned previously, I observe the 5 minute rule when fixing format problems in TinyMCE. If it takes longer than 5 minutes to resolve a formatting/pasting issue, it's better to start over.

By starting over, I do *not* mean deleting the content item and adding a new one. Instead, you can copy your edits into a text editor and start afresh or you can revert to a previous version of the content item before you were experiencing trouble. (See the section called "Reverting to Previous Saves (History)" [104]

If you wish to start fresh, copy your content from the WYSIWYG view of TinyMCE to a text editor, switch to HTML view and delete everything in that window (**Control A** and the **Delete** button). Switch to WYSIWYG view again and paste your original content (still in the text editor) into the text area. Then reintroduce your formatting to the content until it is what you want.

Undoing/Changing Styles in TinyMCE

There are times when you can't undo a style. The reasons for this may depend on which drop-down style was used. Here are ways you can undo the effects of a style.

1. Use the **Control-Z** keystroke combination to undo the most recent actions in your browser.

2. Click the exact same style button twice. The TinyMCE toolbar buttons often act as toggles, so clicking twice will reverse the style you have just applied.

3. Use the **Outdent** style to undo an indent.

4. Choosing a similar style for the same selected passage. If a paragraph or two is centered, the chances are pretty good that if you highlight the same two paragraphs and choose the Left Align option, it will work smoothly. (There is a reason for this; the "center" style and "left" style are mutually exclusive and are added as a class to the <p> tag. That makes it impossible for both styles to be active at once).

5. When changing or undoing a style, make sure that more than one style haven't been applied to the same block of text. This starts to become a

problem if there are two styles being applied to different (but overlapping) parts of the text.

6. Use the **Remove Formatting** button on the toolbar (if visible). Sometimes your Plone site may not have this toolbar button enabled.

7. Manually remove the tags in the HTML code. It is not that difficult to remove an HTML style...just tedious. You may notice that a certain tag surrounds the passage you are trying to style. Usually it is a <p> or <span> or <div> tag (with a class declaration specific to the style). if you are re-moving a style manually this way, be sure to remove the start tag and the finish tag.

Creating Tables with TinyMCE

The buttons on the TinyMCE toolbar contain some functions for making and editing tables. It is functional and comparable to what you see in MS Office or LibreOffice.

Before a table has been created, all TinyMCE buttons related to tables will be grayed out except for the **Insert New Table** button. When you click this, you will be presented with a table configuration menu:

Figure 3.4. Insert/Edit Table

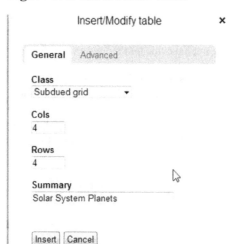

The Class drop-down menu lets you select the table's default style.

After any kind of table has been added and you have placed your cursor inside the table itself, other buttons will be active. These are the standard table buttons which you find in MS Office: *Insert Row Before, Insert Row After, Delete Row, Insert Column Before, Insert Column After, Remove Column, Split Merged Cells, Merge Table Cells.*

Here are a few observations about making tables with Plone:

- If you are already familiar with making HTML tables, it might be easier to create them outside of Plone (i.e., in a text editor) and then paste the html code into TinyMCE. The main advantage of using TinyMCE to make a table is that TinyMCE will apply css classes specific to Plone. However, after you paste the HTML table into TinyMCE, you can still apply these same settings.

- You may notice that the top row is always bold. That is because TinyMCE will specify that the cells will use the *<th>* tag instead of the *<td>* tag. Here Plone is following the convention for most tables.

- **Classes**. This drop-down list lets you choose among different table styles: *Subdued Grid/Invisible Grid/Fancy Listing/.* Any class containing the word "grid" shows the grid lines; the others do not. Your site developers or Admin user might decide to make these classes look different or add additional table styles. (For information about how to do this, see the section called "TinyMCE " [209]).

- The **Advanced Tab** of the Insert/Edit Table dialog lets you set the Table Caption. It will take what you entered in the *Summary* field and put it in a single row at the top (above the heading/TR tags).

- The **Summary** field (corresponding to the summary attribute of the <table> tag) contains table information which is not normally displayed. It is used mainly by screen readers for people who have disabilities.

- Always toggle to full screen mode when editing tables. It is easier.

- To move the cursor to a different cell, use the Up-Down-Left-Right arrow keys on your keyboard. (The tab button on your keyboard does not allow you to move between different table cells).

- To delete a table, you need to go into HTML view and delete the HTML for the table. (i.e., everything between <table> and </table>). It is generally not possible to delete a table in the WYSIWYG view.

- You can add images and hyperlinks within table cells. For this reason, a simple two column or two row table might help with positioning an image or its accompanying caption.

- You can use the handle bars in the borders of the table rows or cells to resize the height or width of a cell or the table as a whole.

- If you leave columns or rows empty after saving, they will not be deleted when you open the document next.

- You know you have done so when the cells/rows/columns are highlighted.

You can set properties for cells and rows. There are two buttons on the TinyMCE toolbar which let you do this.

On the toolbar illustration above, you will notice that certain table-specific styles will become available in the drop-down style list (By the #1 you will see that the style **Heading cell** is being applied). These table styles include: *Subdued Grid, Invisible Grid, Fancy Listing, Fancy Grid Listing, Fancy Vertical Listing, Odd Row, Even Row, Heading Cell*. Applying the Odd Row/Even Row styles to a row will add a class to the row (i.e., <row class="odd">. But that assumes that the site developer has declared tr.odd somewhere in the CSS file). In the default CSS, tr.odd and tr.even are styled to look the same.

Adding Hyperlinks

The TinyMCE toolbar has three buttons for inserting or editing links: Insert/Edit, Unlink and Anchor.

Before discussing how to add links, let's distinguish between external links and internal links.

- An **external link** is a full absolute URL that exists outside of your Plone site. Example: *http://www.google.com*

- An **internal link** is a reference to a URL within the same Plone site. Typically the user makes an internal link in TinyMCE by browsing through Plone content and selecting the item that the internal link should link to.

To create an internal or external link, highlight a portion of the text and click the **Insert/Edit link** icon.

Figure 3.5. The Insert/Edit Link button

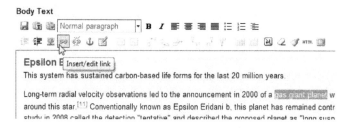

You must highlight some text before the Insert/Edit will become active.

A dialogue will open:

Figure 3.6. Insert/Edit Link Dialog pop-up

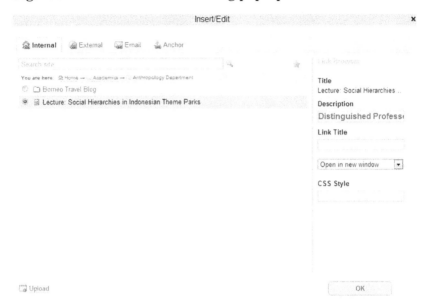

The right panel of the Insert/Edit Link dialog will appear blank until you select something.

Across the top of the pop-up are four tabs:

- **Internal.** Choosing this tab will let you browse for and select links from within your Plone site.

- **External.** This is used for creating external links only.

- **Mail**. This lets you create an email hyperlink. If the visitor clicks on this link, that user's email program will launch with an email addressed to whatever email you choose.

- **Anchors.** Choosing this tab will let you browse for HTML anchors which you have created on this same content item. Unfortunately it does not allow you to locate anchors on other content items.

Adding External Links

To add a conventional external link (http://www.google.com, etc):

1. Highlight a portion of the text and click the **Insert/Edit link** icon.

2. Click the **External** tab on the top of the pop-up dialog).

3. Type or paste the absolute URL into the empty link field. (Note: If you paste the *http://* into the field, Plone will automatically shave it off). If you wish, you can press the *Preview* button to confirm that the URL actually works.

4. *(Optional)* Decide if you wish to complete any of the optional fields (to be discussed below). Click the **Advanced** tab and choose your options (if any).

5. Click the **OK** button at the bottom of your screen. After you do this, the dialog will disappear and you will return to the TinyMCE edit window. The text you originally highlighted should now be underlined as a hyperlink. After you save the content item, the hyperlink should work.

When adding a link, you can include some optional fields. Generally, these fields will not need to be filled out, except in cases where you would like to override default behavior.

• *Link Title*. This differs from the text on the item which is hyperlinked. The link title provides additional information especially helpful for the visually impaired. For most people, the text in the link title (which actually is the *title* attribute of the <a> element) appears as a tool tip when you hover over it. In special cases, this can be helpful, but users don't normally expect to see this extra information.

• *Open in this window/frame, Open in New Window, Open in Parent Window/Frame, Open in Top Window (replaces all frame)*. Almost always you should leave this **blank** and just use the site defaults. This option lets you override the site defaults for this one link.

• *CSS Style*. There appears to be a field to add small amounts of CSS. When I tried this feature in Chrome 28 and Firefox 22, it appeared not to work. Keep in mind that even if this field did work, the site's HTML filtering will automatically strip all CSS declarations except those which are explicitly allowed in its HTML list. (The Admin user can tweak these settings by going to *Site Setup --> HTML Filtering --> Styles Tab*).

Using Internal Links

An internal link is a link to another page on the same Plone site.

Advantages of using internal links

Even though making an internal link is slightly more complicated than just pasting a URL, using them helps maintain the site over the long term.

This is because Plone uses **link integrity** to ensure that internal links don't go bad.

Linkrot (the tendency for Internet links to break after a certain period of time) is a perennial problem. One cannot control whether URLs on third party sites go bad, but Plone monitors whether internal links (i.e., links to other parts of the same site) are still valid. When content creators use the rich text editor, they are given a choice to either create an external link or an internal link. Previously, it was simpler for content creators just to paste the URL (regardless of whether the URL was an internal link or an external one). Now though, the editor interface has been designed specifically to encourage content creators to create an internal link to a URL on the same website rather than just pasting the URL. Plone's link integrity checker will detect when you are trying to delete something required by another web page. By notifying you before you delete the item, you are given the opportunity to remove the expiring link or to change it (or contact the appropriate person to take action).

Figure 3.7. Link Integrity pop-up

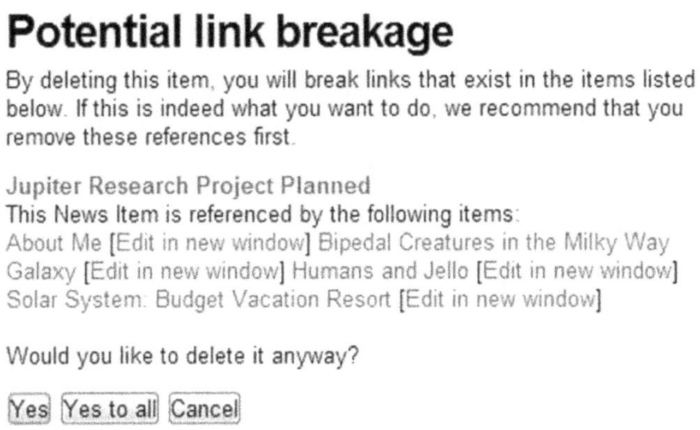

Potential link breakage

By deleting this item, you will break links that exist in the items listed below. If this is indeed what you want to do, we recommend that you remove these references first.

Jupiter Research Project Planned
This News Item is referenced by the following items:
About Me [Edit in new window] Bipedal Creatures in the Milky Way
Galaxy [Edit in new window] Humans and Jello [Edit in new window]
Solar System: Budget Vacation Resort [Edit in new window]

Would you like to delete it anyway?

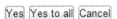

Before you delete a content item, Plone will warn you if other content items are currently linking to it.

Internal links also protect you if the site is reorganized and the content is moved into different folders on the site. Plone makes that easy; if an internal link has been correctly added, Plone will redirect the viewer from the expired URL to the more recent URL. A page link may still use the original URL, but Plone will know to forward it to the right one. From the perspective of system maintenance, using internal links whenever possible substantially reduces the amount of linkrot.

Oddly, when an item is moved from one Plone folder to another, internal links which were manually added as *Related Items* by the content creator may not move successfully. If these content items had Related Items associated with them, the content creator may need to add them manually later.

Adding Internal Links

The biggest challenge about internal links is finding and selecting the correct link among the list of possible pages. Remember that Plone uses the metaphor of folders and files. Therefore you need to browse up or down the hierarchy of content to find the internal link you want. It also requires an awareness of your location in the Plone site and that of the page you wish to link to.

The dialog window has 4 tabs: *External*, *Internal*, *Email* and *Anchor*. The first tab *Internal* shows the contents of the current folder. Note: This includes all the contents (subfolders, images, etc.) It also includes a "breadcrumbs" trail of parent folders to let you navigate easily through other folders.

Underneath the tabs are two things: a search box and a gold star. The Search box lets you find an internal link by typing in a title or keyword. Clicking the gold star will reveal additional locations (usually *Home* and *Current Folder*). The Admin user can select additional locations in this same spot (Go to *Site Setup -- > TinyMCE --> Content Browser*).

Generally, the search feature works well in the Insert/Edit link dialog. However, if you are having problems locating the item you wish to create an internal link to, open a separate window and search there (or better yet, use the Advanced Search – see the section called "Advanced Search " [188]). Once you have found the right item using this method (and know the title, or description), it should be relatively easy to search for the appropriate internal link within the pop-up.

Tips for Finding Internal Items:

- You can only link to the item after it has been published. If it has not been published, you should be the owner or have knowledge of when it will be published.

- When browsing through internal links in the pop-up, clicking once on an image will reveal a preview in the right panel.

Linking to the Middle of the Page (Anchors)

An anchor is a concept in HTML that allows you to link to a position midway down a web page. The Edit toolbar contains a button which lets you create an invisible anchor in the HTML code. You will be prompted to give it a name, and then it is done. Once the anchor is added, you can add links to it anywhere within the same content item by highlighting the text you'd like to link, clicking the

"Insert/Edit Link" button, and going to "Anchor" in the top bar. From there, a list of available anchors will appear. Simple!

Be sure to give the anchor a meaningful name. **Note**: Anchors are not reciprocal; adding an anchor to a location within the page will allow you to add as many links as you'd like that will bring you to that anchor, but you cannot click the anchor to return to the link location. Adding a second anchor to the same location as the first will remove the first anchor, but not the links to it. This will lead to broken hyperlinks that have no reference.

Unfortunately the pop-up dialog which lets you browse for links no longer allows you to look up anchors on other content items. That makes it harder to keep track of anchors on other pages. (You may even need to look at the raw HTML to find out the name of the anchor).

Autogenerating a hyperlinked Table of Contents at the top of the page

You can also autogenerate a Table of Contents at the top of the page. For this to work, you must use headings and subheadings to divide your page into sections. For more information, see the section called "Autogenerating a hyperlinked Table of Contents at the top of the page" [66].

Using Anchors to Make Endnotes

Endnotes have fallen out of favor on the Internet, but they still have an important role to play. If you have checked Wikipedia recently, you will know the reason. Many external links which were added are now dead. Sometimes, valuable information is available online in an offline source like a book or print newspaper. Wikipedia made a decision a few years ago to require that the main text body of their articles link to footnotes at the bottom. The endnotes themselves would contain the hyperlinks to the third party sources.

That is generally a good practice. First, it allows the page citing the source to include bibliographic information in an unobtrusive manner on the bottom of the page. Second, it gives the reader more clues for finding the original source if the third party source has gone offline or if the URL has changed. Sometimes, when the URL has changed on a third party link, if you know the title or some identifying keywords, it can be relatively easy to find the new line if it is still online. Sometimes it is just helpful to keep information about the source on the same page for the reader's convenience.

While HTML has made it easy to create links to external sources, making endnotes is clumsy and time-consuming (even for people relatively comfortable with

HTML). Perhaps the concept of the endnotes does not translate well to the browser page; nonetheless, with the use of anchors, Plone can simplify the process somewhat of creating and maintaining them.

The process in Plone is very easy. At the bottom of your article/page, add an anchor to each endnote. Then return to the main text body and add links using the anchor you have just created. Highlight the note label, choose Insert/Edit link, choose the Anchor tab at the top and select the anchor which you have already created. The only complicated part is creating a style for Subscript/Superscript and manually numbering the endnote numbers.

I don't want to oversell this functionality on Plone. It certainly does not compare in functionality with reference management software like EndNote or Zotero. But its ease of making, storing and referencing anchors makes it a good cheap-and-dirty solution for someone wishing to add endnotes or even footnotes to a relatively simple document.

Adding Images and Files from TinyMCE

Adding images to accompany text for a content item is a common task for the content creator. The process for adding images within the TinyMCE editor is almost identical to the process for uploading files through TinyMCE, so we will cover both tasks together. First, we will talk about how to upload images. In the previous discussion about adding links within TinyMCE, there is greater detail on how to upload content that can be linked.

There are two ways to upload files to Plone. First, by adding a File content type to whatever folder you are in. Second, by using the *Upload* option in the rich text editor. (There is a third way which will not be discussed here; it involves using a third party desktop tool to upload multiple files into Plone. The Plone community has developed a few uploading tools for doing this).

Uploading Method One: Adding a file to the current folder

1. Close the page you are editing or go up to the folder containing the page.

2. From the **Add New** drop-down list, choose **File.** If you do not see this option, that may mean that this item type cannot be added here, but sometimes it is merely temporarily hidden in the *More* drop-down option. By selecting the *More* option, you can determine whether the File item type is forbidden or just hidden. (For more, see the section called "Where can I add content? " [56]).

3. Give the file a meaningful name and upload it. Make sure the file is not hidden. (Generally if the folder containing it is public, the file will be public as well).

4. Now return to the original page you were editing.

Uploading Method Two: Upload a file or image through the TinyMCE Editor

Why would you ever want to upload a file (like a PDF file) using TinyMCE? Because you usually will upload a PDF or MS Word file for the sake of linking to it, it makes sense just to add a link and then upload the item at the same time you wish to link to it.

As long as you have the right to add a file to a folder, you can also upload it through the TinyMCE editor. This applies both for the case where you are uploading an image and uploading a file like a PDF.

Note: If you have navigated into folders where you don't have the rights to add items, the upload button will not appear to work. You will be able to browse for the file on your computer, but the upload button may be disabled. This is intentional and merely reflects that Plone's permission system is working correctly.

The process for uploading a file or image through TinyMCE are practically the same.

Figure 3.8. Uploading Things through TinyMCE

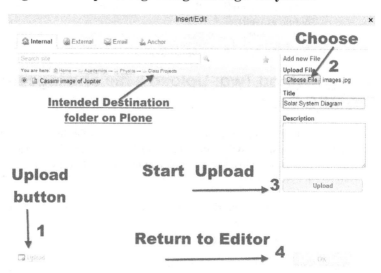

After you push the Start Upload button (3), Plone will display the uploaded image & allow you to set properties to it.

The basic steps are:

1. When inside the text editor, select the **Image** button or the **Hyperlink** button. (*Note:* the hyperlink button will not be active until you select a word or phrase in the text). In the resulting pop-up, make sure that the Plone folder browser (in the middle) is at the place where you'd like the file to be uploaded. Typically, the safest bet is to use the same folder you are currently in. Fortunately, that's the default.

2. Click the **Upload** button on bottom left of the pop-up. Click the **Choose File** button and search for the file you wish to upload on your computer.

3. Click the **Upload** button (on the right panel). This will start the upload and show additional settings related to the uploaded file (and possibly a preview).

4. Configure these additional settings. (They will be described in detail below). When you are ready to return to the text editor in the main browser window, click the **OK** button on the bottom right.

If you are uploading an image, the following options will appear on the right panel after you have uploaded.

If you know that the file has already been added to Plone site and wish merely to create a hyperlink to it, the steps for doing so are similar to adding an internal link.

1. Return to the content item in TinyMCE and highlight the word or phrase you wish to be the link to the downloadable file. Example: **Employment Application (PDF)**.

2. Highlight the words of the label and select the **Insert/Edit** link button.

3. Browse for the PDF file as you would for an image or page item.

4. When you find the right PDF item, select it and press the **Insert** button.

At this point you will be able to see a link in your page going straight to the file you just uploaded. **Note:** the URL will not end in PDF but the title of the file you named when you uploaded it.

To find out more information about the file content item, see the section called "Files" [73].

Removing Hyperlinks

By default the TinyMCE editor includes an **Unlink** button that will remove a hyperlink on the page. Things to note:

• You should highlight the exact phrase of the hyperlink you wish to unlink. If you have highlighted more than the phrase, this action will neutralize all hyperlinks within that highlighted area.

• The bigger complication is highlighting less than the original phrase in the hyperlink. If you do that and select Unlink, what you selected will no longer be hyperlinked, but the remaining fragment of the original hyperlink which you failed to select will still be a hyperlink. Be careful. It is easy to include a period or comma in the original hyperlink, and then when you Unlink the phrase, the period or comma will still be a hyperlink. This can distract users.

• Sometimes the Undo command (Control-Z) can restore the hyperlink if you accidentally press the Unlink button. As a last resort, you could also revert to a previous version temporarily to find what the original link was. See the section called "Reverting to Previous Saves (History)" [104] .

Adding Images

The ability to add images to your page is by now a standard feature on content management systems, web-based email and even Facebook. Naturally, the rich-text editor in Plone includes a way to add images to your content item.

The pop-up dialog for adding images looks almost the same as that for uploading files/adding internal links. You have two choices: to browse for an existing image on the Plone site, or to upload your image immediately.

To upload an image, simply click the **Upload** button when the Image pop-up dialog appears. After it is successfully uploaded, you can change the size, the Link Title, write captions or write a description (which will appear as a value in the alt attribute of the image element). Here are a few non-intuitive details worth keeping in mind:

- After the images appear in the editor window, you can grab the handles of the image and use them to increase or decrease the size of the image.

- Because images typically have no workflow, whether they are published depends on whether the containing folder is published. That means you will be able to find and link to images uploaded by other users. (If your site has configured the image item type to have a workflow, this may not be true. See Chapter 8, *Collaborative Editing: Workflows* [129]).

- You can align the image on the page by selecting the image and then pressing the Left/Center/Right justify button on the edit toolbar. Selecting **left** will allow text to float around the image on the right. Selecting **right** will allow text to float around the image on the left. Selecting **inline** will have the image interrupt the flow of text and prevent floating. Generally, you should select Left or Right.

- Uploading images through the TinyMCE button is not the only way to upload images into Plone. You can also upload images through the **Add New** drop-down option on the top right bar. This was discussed earlier. Images are also one of the standard Plone content types and are covered in greater detail in the section called "Images" [71].

To make the image itself into a hyperlink to another web page:

1. Drop the image into the content item using the Image toolbar.

2. Exit the Image dialog. Click on the image in the Edit window. You should be able to see handles at the edges of the image which you can grab or select.

3. Select the whole image and select the **Insert/Edit** button on the Edit toolbar.

4. Add your hyperlink as you would normally and then press **Update/Ok**.

Adding Multimedia

There is no standard way to add multimedia into TinyMCE. The generic Plone does not allow you to use the code for embedding YouTube links for example. There are two reasons for this. First, the embedding code provided by sites like YouTube contain elements like <object> which are stripped out of TinyMCE. This is done mainly for security reasons. The Admin user can modify these settings on the HTML filtering menu in Site Setup (See the section called "HTML Filtering " [204]). Second, the layout dimensions or the stylings of an embedded video may conflict with the site's design or layout, and Plone wants to make sure that incompatible styling isn't allowed to be shown.

The implementation of embedded video varies between different Plone sites. You will need to check with your site developer or planner about the best way to do this on your organization's site. Here are some possibilities:

- Some Plone sites may require you to first add the video link outside of the rich text editor by selecting **Add New --> Link** from the folder. After you do that, you will open the rich text editor, choose **Insert/Edit Media** from TinyMCE. This function is an optional icon on the TinyMCE toolbar. If you can see the Insert/Edit Media icon on your toolbar, that generally is a good sign that you can add an embedded video this way (although it is by no means guaranteed).

- Some Plone sites may ask that you simply create a hyperlink to the You-Tube video from within TinyMCE. The hyperlink code would look something like this: `<a href="http://www.you-tube.com/watch?v=K2cYWfq--Nw">video </a>` . After doing this, Plone will automatically add the embedding code for you.

- Some Plone sites may in fact allow you to paste the embedded code in HTML view. **Note:** If your site does not allow the adding of video by this method, you may sometimes still see the YouTube video when in WYSI-WYG/edit mode of the TinyMCE before you press Submit. If this embedded video disappears after you press the Submit button, that means that the HTML filtering settings have removed or disabled your HTML code.

- Some Plone sites may actively discourage the use of embedded videos from appearing on a Plone content page. In this case, the only option for a content creator is to link to the YouTube video as though it were a simple hyperlink.

- On Plone.org there is a Plone tutorial called "How to Embed Flickr, YouTube, or MySpace Content" which covers this topic in more detail. The URL can be found at the section called "Other Places to Find Help " [6]

Adding Wiki Links in TinyMCE

Wikis are becoming more popular, and some Plone sites may have set aside areas of the website which allow for communal editing.

TinyMCE already has implemented the ability to make internal links and add images. Plone also has implemented a very basic ability to add a conditional link which logged in users can expand upon by clicking it. All you need to do is add double parentheses around the word or phrase that you wish to make a conditional link:

```
Al Gore is a leading advocate of ((climate change le-
gislation))and won the ((Nobel Peace Prize)) for his
efforts.
```

After pressing submit, you will see that the double parentheses produce conditional or wikified links around the topics "climate change legislation" and "Nobel Peace Prize." **Note:** Attempting to add a wiki link to an embedded image will cause the image link to break, as well as create an unformatted Page with the name of the broken link.

Figure 3.9. How wiki links are rendered

After you add double parentheses around a word or phrase, a plus sign will cause a new page to be created.

This functionality is not turned on by default. The Admin user may need to turn is feature on. See the section called "Enabling Wiki Markup" [206].

Tweaking the TinyMCE Settings (Admins only)

The Admin user has access to a configuration screen for modifying some of the TinyMCE Settings (*See the section called "TinyMCE " [209].*) This includes settings for:

- resizing the editing window

- adding/removing edit toolbar buttons

- adding custom styles on the style drop-down menu

- disabling/enabling the TinyMCE context menu.

Changing or Disabling the Rich Text Editor

Users can temporarily or permanently turn off the rich text editor. To do this:

1. Click on your user name at the top right corner of your browser.

2. Choose the drop-down option called **Preferences**.

3. On the WYSIWYG editor options, you will see a drop-down list of options. Choose **None**.

This can be helpful if you are trying to transfer lots of legacy content which are text files or restructured text or if you have been encountering some problems with the HTML filter in Plone.

Other Ways to Add & Edit Content

Although TinyMCE is the preferred tool to add and edit content in Plone, there are other methods:

- **External Editor.** This is a desktop tool that allows you to do local editing. It is difficult to configure right, but some swear by it. Personally, I have found it more trouble than it's worth.

- **Webdav clients like Enfold Desktop.** When I worked for Enfold Systems, I used their free tool Enfold Desktop. It's especially good for uploading multiple files and moving things within the same site. It's also fairly easy to set up. But it's not especially helpful for editing; sometimes it would be difficult figuring out which HTML code would be filtered or stripped. Webdav clients are the most helpful for uploading multiple files (like images) into a single folder without using the web browser.

- **No editor at all!** You can turn off TinyMCE for one item, or all the time. (See the section called "Getting Your Bearings" [7]). This is useful if you already have clean HTML code and don't want TinyMCE to mess with it. Remember though that Plone uses an HTML Filter to filter out various HTML and CSS code, so Plone could conceivably zap away some illegal tags from your HTML. My experience so far has been that pasting code into the HTML Window of TinyMCE works well enough, so there never been a need to disable it.

One reason for these alternate methods is to make the editing process less dependent on a web browser, which can be prone to crashing. Another reason was that it used to be impossible to revert to earlier versions of a content item. Since then, TinyMCE has become more reliable, and the optional Save button on the TinyMCE toolbar makes it easy to do multiple saves when editing content. Because Plone keeps a version history of all past saves, it is now a simple matter to revert to a previous version of an item.

Editing Page Properties

When you open the Edit screen, other options are available on the Edit tab above the TinyMCE toolbar. You might think they are controlled by TinyMCE, but in fact they are general properties for the item type you are editing. These properties will be covered in greater detail in Chapter 4, *Item Types* [56].

Chapter 4. Item Types

Plone allows you to add a variety of content types for your site, and by default, Plone includes several generic content types. It is also easy to create a new content type, since new content types are often based on generic content types, with modifications to one or two different fields or properties. Keep in mind that your organization's Plone site may contain different (or unfamilar) content types that have already been customized to the organization. Once you are familiarized with how the default content types work, it will be much easier to understand how they are customized to an organization.

The generic content types for Plone 4: are Pages, Events, News, Images, Folders, Link, News Item, File and Collection.

This chapter will cover Pages, Events, News, Images, Link, News Item and Files.

The next chapter will cover two content items which can contain other content items: Folders and Collections.

Note: The first part of this chapter will cover properties and behavior which are common to *all* content types.

Where can I add content?

Unlike some content management systems (which require clicking a button to add a post or page), you can add content in Plone only at certain locations.

You can add content only inside a folder

We will cover the folder content type (and collections) in the next chapter. A folder is a container for other content types. In other words, a folder can contain pages, files, images and even other folders. The default view for a folder may be customized but it generally shows you all items contained inside this folder.

In general, assuming that your user account has the right permissions, you can only add new content inside a folder (or any folderish content type). When your browser is at a folder and you have permissions to add content into this folder, you will see the **Add New** option at the top of your content area. You must be at a folder (or similar content type) to be able to see this screen.

Figure 4.1. Adding Items to a Folder

If you see the Add new option on the toolbar, that is almost certainly a sign that you are currently viewing a folder

Configuring Properties for Item Types

As you work with Plone, you'll soon realize that different content types share many of the same properties. This section will describe these properties, which are generally found in all content types (and even for customized content types). Later, when we cover each content type, we will describe properties that are unique to it.

Regardless of content type, an item usually has three displays:

- **View**. This is how the content item will appear to anonymous site visitors.

- **Edit**. This display lets you edit the content item.

- **Sharing**. This display lets you view (and sometimes edit) the users or groups who can edit the content item.

A fourth display type, Contents, appears only for folders and folder-like objects:

- **Contents** (*this appears only for folder content types*). This display lets you decide how the items in the container are arranged.

Depending on user permissions, you may be able to see one, two, or all of these displays. You can switch from one view to the other simply by clicking the appropriate tab on the content bar. *Note:* if you are editing, your changes will be lost if you click to another tab like View or Sharing. You will need to save first. To save time, one easy way to switch back and forth from different views is to keep the same item open in different browsers. For example, you could be simultaneously editing the content item in Firefox, viewing it as a logged in user in Chrome, and also viewing it as an anonymous visitor in Internet Explorer. Every time you make a change, you can hit the F5 Refresh button to see how it appears.

View Display

The "View" display presents items just as they will appear to anonymous visitors. Keep it mind that it will not look exactly the same as the view for an editor or a logged-in user. While editing for example, you may see portlets to the side of the page which an anonymous visitor will not see (once these portlets are gone, that could conceivably affect the width of the display). Anonymous visitors will also not see the drop-down actions and login information that would normally be visible to a content creator.

How a display appears will vary by item type. For example, a Page will generally show the title, description and a body of text, while an Event will show the time and place relevant to the event. The views of all item types will have a number of elements in common:

Figure 4.2. View display for Page

Solar System: Budget Vacation Resort

by Dick Solomon — last modified Jul 23, 2010 01:03 PM — History

Impressions about a charming provincial planet called Earth in the Solar System.

If you are headed over to Luyten's Star to view the famed Soaring Eyeball exhibit and need to take a pit stop, you couldn't do worse than to stop at the Solar System.

The Solar System has a beautiful asteroid belt, a ringed planet and three inhabited moons. Only one planet (called Earth) is inhabited, and its atmosphere is generally breathable (but infested with all kinds of carcinogens, so don't forget to activate your air filter).

The planet has clean restrooms and great museums. Particularly recommended: MacDonalds Fast Food Restaurant, Walmart and any sports stadium.

The bipedal creatures on Earth (called "humans") are generally friendly, but only speak one or two languages and rarely travel off their planet.

Key Phrases

- "How's it shaking, man?" General form of address before you ask directions.
- "My name is Marvin(Marlene); what's yours?" Humans don't have identity sensors, so they associate each living creature with a spoken sound which is supposed to identify the person. Humans generally don't care what your name is, as long as the gender is correct.

Recreational Activities

Humans are a diverse bunch and have a variety of recreational activities unrelated to eating, intercourse or waste disposal. Examples:

- Moving in shallow pools of water where they cannot breathe.
- Complaining about politics. On Earth, there is no taboo against complaining about political leaders. (This characteristic is generally found in primitive societies before brains were implanted with thought-surveillance devices). As a result, humans often complain about political systems over which they have no control.

‹ Previous: Milky Way Stars   Next: Astronomy Club Meeting ›

History will not be shown to anonymous visitors.

In the above screenshot, the highlighted box would *not* appear for anonymous site visitors – only for users with edit permission for the content item. In the illustration above, note the elements which are displayed:

1. **Breadcrumbs** are a series of hyperlinks at the top of the page, above the content bar, and generally appear to anonymous and logged-in users.

2. **Byline** contains the author's name and link to the History function. (*Note:* The History link will be missing when viewed by anonymous visitors. Also, there is an option in *Site Options --> Security* to disable bylines altogether for anonymous visitors).

3. **Summary**. The text entered in the Summary field will appear in a different font style from the main text. This summary also appears in the <META> section in the HTML head.

4. **Next/Previous navigation links** (whether this appears will depend on the properties for the folder which contains this item).

The Edit display

Generally, you will choose the Edit tab on the content bar to edit an item. The Edit tab will appear only if you have rights to edit the item. After you select the Edit tab, you will generally see three things:

- The content minibar (marked as #1 in the illustration below).

- Middle of Screen: the editing screen (usually the rich text editor) for the Default view.

- The Save button, along with a Change Note field (if versioning has been enabled).

Figure 4.3. The Default view in Editing mode

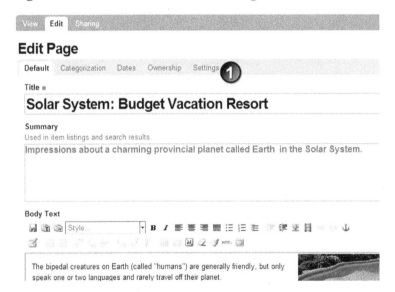

After you select the Edit tab, the content minibar (marked with the number 1) will appear. You can switch between tabs of the content minibar without needing to save.

The content minibar contains five additional tabs which you can choose while editing content:

- Default

- Categorization

- Dates

- Ownership

- Settings

When you reach the Edit screen, Plone will take you first to the Default tab. Unlike the content tab, it is *not* necessary to save your content before switching from one tab to another of the content minibar. That is because the fields under these five tabs are all associated with the same content item; when you save, you are saving the values for all the fields, not just what are editing in the rich text editor.

The other four tabs (Categorization, Dates, Ownership, Settings) contain fields which are generic and thus can be found on more than one content type. Many relate to metadata for search purposes. Often you will not need to fill out all the fields, but it is important to remember what options exist.

Default Component

Title. For each item, choose a short but revealing title, which relates directly to the item's content. Because Plone uses titles for navigation purposes, carefully choosing your titles will make it much easier to find things on the site. Well-chosen titles also help your pages to receive higher ratings from search engines and make them more easily discovered by potential visitors. *Note:* Image and File content types do not need to have a Title.

Summary. It is vital to choose a summary because they appear in search results and automatically-generated views (such as folders and collections).

For some items (and especially container types like Collections and Folders), there may be little to edit on the default tab.

Categorization Component

On this tab you can select tags or related content which aid in browsing or findability on the site's search engines.

Tags   Tags in Plone serve as another way of marking content, and site visitors will also be able to browse through the content items by their associated tags.

To Add New Tags: On the Categorization tab, there is a form field where you can start adding your tags. Click anywhere on the **New Tags** rectangle and start typing your tags, one per line. Keep in mind that tags can be comprised of multiple words, but you can only put one tag on each line. After you select save, and go back to the Categorization tab, you have the option of checking or unchecking the tags you have just created. You can select zero tags, or multiple tags for a content item you are editing. *Note:* You must have at least the Admin user or Reviewer role to be able to add new tags, and the Reviewer can only add tags if the state is Pending.

You cannot prevent tags from appearing on the tag list unless the Admin user has unchecked this tag from every content item. This actually is not as hard to verify as it sounds. Just click the hyperlink for the tag to see how many other items have been given the same tag. Alternatively, you can create a Collection which finds all instances of this tag appearing on a content item. Then just go to each item appearing on this list and uncheck the tag you wish to remove. As soon as no content items are using this tag, the tag in question will disappear from the tag list.

If your website has been active for a longer period of time, there will probably already be a variety of tags to choose from. For strategies on how to use tags on your site, see the section called " Use tags effectively " [179].

Related Items

You can choose to associate the current content item with another one. Click the **Add** button. You will see a pop-up dialog similar to the Insert/edit dialogue in TinyMCE. (See the section called "Adding Hyperlinks " [41].

How the related content will appear to site visitors depends on the layout and design of your web site. By default, it appears after the main content, with the heading **Related content**.

To delete a link, deselect the checkmark next to it and save the form. *Important Note*: If you are moving or copying the item to another folder on the site, it will break all the internal links you have included on Related Items. You will need to add them again manually.

Location

You can associate the content item to a geographical location here. There are a number of add-on products for Plone that can utilize this geographical information. One such use is that all the geographic data can be represented visually on on a map of the world.

Language   Using this menu, you can select the language in which the item is written. Which language is set as the default will depend upon how your website is configured.

Dates Component

The "Dates" part of the form allows you to set a duration of time for which the content is publicly visible.

Publishing Date   This is where you can specify the date from which the item is visible to the public. Even if the item in question has been through the workflow process and received a "Published" state, it still will not be visible to the public until the publishing date has been reached.

Expiration Date   If an expiration date has been entered, the item at hand will no longer be visible to the public after that date.

Together, these two entries constitute the "Date Available" entry in the Dublin Core standard.

A few notes:

- If you do not choose a date here, when the state has been changed to Published, it will be published immediately and never expire.

- If you are submitting your content item for review, it may be preferable not to specify any dates and let the Reviewer specify the date and duration of the content. The main exception would be time-sensitive items like Events (which no longer need to be shown after the date has passed).

- Despite the fact that there is a field for hour and minute, you can just leave this blank. (By default, Plone will assume that the Publishing Date will be 12:00 AM).

- If for some reason your content item has not been published even though it is supposed to, chances are that the internal clock of the web server is not synchronized with the clock of the person creating the content. (That is yet another reason to let the Reviewer take care of scheduling).

- The *Advanced* option of the Workflow State drop-down menu (which is on the top right of the Plone toolbar) will let the submitter or reviewer schedule a publish date. Because delays are inevitable in any publishing process, it might be better for the reviewer to be the one specifying the publishing and expiration date.

Ownership Component

In the "Ownership" component you can enter copyright information for the item and list the names of people who helped with the content.

Creators
Enter one or more user names. In order to include any number of people, enter each of their names onto a separate line in the "Creators" field.

Contributors
This is where you can enter the real names of any other people who made a contribution to the item. Here again, use a single line for each name. How you distinguish these two groups is not a technical issue but an editing one. Creators are generally thought of as people who were involved in creating the item on the website. Contributors are usually people who have made contributions or additions to the item but who have not actually added it to the website. They may not even be registered on the website at all.

Rights
In this field, you can issue a Creative Commons License or reserve all rights. This field may already be filled out by your administrator. This is also the appropriate place to inform third parties about copyright status.

How this information appears is customized to the site's needs. For example, the byline is usually reserved for the name of the user who created the content for the first time. Some Plone sites will have templates that show the names of all creators and contributors. Some sites will not list this information at all. The information you are entering here serves two primary purposes: 1) values for Dublin Core metadata (which will be embedded on web pages, but will not be visible to site visitors) and 2) values for fields which can be added for custom templates.

Settings Component

The options which appear here depend on the content item you are currently editing. However, these two options generally appear for all content items:

Allow comments
Your item can be configured to allow comments from logged in or anonymous users. If for some reason this option doesn't work, ask a user with the Manager role to verify that comments are globally enabled. Just because you have enabled comments on a content doesn't mean that you have the right to approve these comments. If comments are moderated, you will need to have Re-

viewer rights on that item to be able to see comments in the moderation queue. For more about Plone's commenting infrastructure, see the section called "Configuring Comments " [190].

Exclude from navigation

Depending on your pre-settings, certain item types will appear in the navigation portlet or among the main navigation tabs. You can use this option to exclude an item from both of these displays.

The Admin user may have already set global defaults for a content item. See the chapter about the section called "Types" [212]. But you can still override the global settings from this screen.

Pages

The presentation of a Page can be altered using headings, text-formatting tools, links, images, and a variety of other tools at your disposal.

When entering text, it is best to use the rich-text editor. TinyMCE makes it easy to do basic page layout and styling. It presents the text to you just as it will later appear in the view display of the Page. Additionally, it provides you with the most important functions offered by ordinary word processing programs. For more about this editor, see Chapter 3: "*The Rich Text Editor*" (page 21).

If you do not use the rich-text editor, you will find a simple form field in its place, which you can use to enter unformatted text, HTML code, or a simplified text markup language such as Restructured Text, Markdown, or Textile. Plone transforms all entries into valid HTML.

Below, we will explore the options and modes which are exclusive to the Page content type:

Using Presentation Mode with a Page

One option in Edit Page (Settings) lets you make a page viewable in a web browser as a presentation. To enable this feature, check **Presentation Mode**. This feature is not intended to replace PowerPoint, but it provides a simple way of showing outlines in a web browser as a series of slides. After you enable this option, a link will then appear in the page's view display under the description: "**Also available**

in presentation mode..." In presentation mode, the page's content will be divided into full-screen pages, which are ordered consecutively.

Technically speaking, presentation mode is nothing more than the view display combined with presentation commands based on the S5 system. You can learn more about S5 at **http://meyerweb.com/eric/tools/s5/**.

This Presentation Mode has limited features and is intended only for simple presentations. Also, your content must be organized as an outline. That means:

- Use **Headings** on the Style drop-down list each time you wish to begin a new slide. A subheading will appear as a title for a slide.

- Anything formatted like regular paragraphs will not show up in presentation mode.

- Under each heading, you should use ordered lists, unordered lists and definition lists to indicate an outline for your presentation.

- Images and tables will appear as normal.

- Sentences which are styled by the **Highlight** style in the drop-down style list will also appear.

- Font formatting (bold, italics, align center) will generally display in presentation mode.

Autogenerating a hyperlinked Table of Contents at the top of the page

For longer text areas involving numerous subheadings, Plone can automatically generate a table of contents at the beginning of the page item, containing links to the individual sections of the same page. Essentially you are autogenerating HTML anchors at each place where you have a heading and subheading on the same page.

It's easy to do.

1. Click on the **Settings** tab and check the **Table of Contents** option.

2. Divide your contents into sections that represent logical divisions of the content.

3. Separate each section with a line break.

4. At each line break, type an appropriate title for each section.

5. Select a title and apply the **Heading** or **Subheading** style from the drop-down style list. *Note:* for the hyperlinks to generate properly, you must start with a Heading style.

6. Apply a style for each section title in the same way. There's no rule about how to do this, but be consistent and try to maintain an overall hierarchy. A subordinate section (marked by the Subheading) should be listed under a section marked with a Heading.

7. Press **Save**.

After you escape from the editing screen and view the content item normally, you will see an embedded Table of Contents.

Figure 4.4. Autogenerated Table of Contents

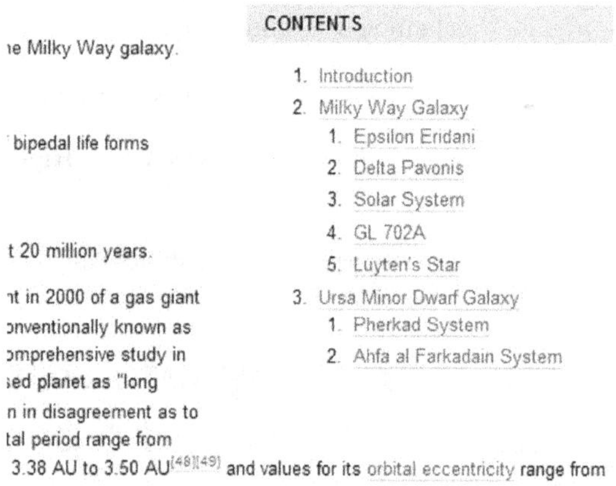

Tip: Start with the Heading drop-down style whenever autogenerating a Table of Contents

Note: When you create a Table of Contents this way, TinyMCE will put anchors at each position which you marked as Heading or Subheading. These anchors will be visible when you try to link to them using the Insert link button for this page. The Insert Link dialog will list the available anchor links on that same content item from the **Anchor** tab.

News Items

The news item content type is similar to the page item type, and has the following characteristics:

- News have an extra field for adding an image. Adding an image is optional. The image you add through this field has nothing to do with the images you can insert into an item's text using TinyMCE, and will appear alongside the News item in the News folder View.

- Default Plone installations usually have a News folder at the root level which appears as a tab on the top of a page. When a site visitor clicks this tab, he or she will see a list of the latest published news items. When viewing the News tab, you will see the Title, Summary and the image which you added.

- Because the Summary will appear on the news page, it is important to create a meaningful summary for each news item. It should be one or two sentences long.

- You should choose a tag for a News item that indicates a category of news or a relevant department. This will make it easier to use Collections to group similar kinds of News items.

There is a special News portlet which shows only News items. In fact, using a News portlet can be the ideal way for site visitors to be informed about general news for site visitors. (See the section called the section called "News Portlets" [171] for more information.

On the other hand, a news portlet will show all of a site's news item regardless of subject matter. Therefore, it is intended for news items of relevance to all site visitors.

Or suppose you want your portlet to show only news items relating to one department, or only sports-related announcements. How would you do that?

1. Ensure that your News items are properly tagged. A News item for the physics department should have an intuitive tag like "physics" or "physics department."

2. Create a Collection query to find all News items having the "physics" tag.

3. Inside the physics folder (or the section of the site for the physics department), add a Collection portlet. This portlet will use the Collection you just created.

It is possible to make an RSS feed out of News items. In fact, the initial News tab in a default Plone installation already has an accompanying RSS feed because the tab URL is actually a Collection (and Collections can have RSS feeds associated with them). For more information, see the section called "Making and Customizing Web Feeds " [195]

Timeliness. Unlike a Page (which is presumed to be interesting and relevant long after publication), a news item will stay fresh for only a certain period of time. The site visitor probably expects to be able to view the most recent News items first and yet also be able to access an archive of older news item as well. (That may depend on your organization and the way your organization uses the site). For this reason, it is not usually necessary to set an expiration date for the news item. Sometimes a Content Rule is used to move News items into a different location for archived material.

Should you hide the News Item from the Add New drop-down list? The News item has a specific function on a site, but it might confuse content creators who are unfamiliar with Plone terminology. From a metaphysical perspective, almost any new content item could be regarded as "news." One way to handle this confusion is for the Admin user to hide this file type from popular directories or even rename the file type altogether.

Events

The accuracy of the time listed on an Event item is of paramount importance. Since an Event item announces activities on a particular date, such as meetings or seminars, it is important that the time listed is accurate. Most visitors are only interested in these events before they occur, not after they have passed. Take care when filling in information such as start and end dates, and start and end times of the event, the event location, and details concerning a contact person. This event-related information can be entered into individual fields on the Edit page for Event items and is then saved in structured form, allowing Plone to use it directly.

Just as with Pages, Event items possess a field for the title, description, and main text body. You will edit the contents of the main text body using the rich text editor.

The event item also contains these fields:

Event Location	the location of the event or place of meeting
Event Starts/Event Ends	the time frame in which the event is to take place (*Required*)
Attendees	a list of expected participants
Event Type(s)	choose one or more categories or add a new one.

Event URL	an Internet address for further information (*Note that while this field will attempt to validate links, it will only do so if the string "http" has been omitted at the beginning of the link.*)
Contact Name	name of a contact person who is responsible for answering any questions concerning the event (*Note: The contact name will not need to be a username.*)
Contact Address	the contact person's e-mail address
Contact Phone	the contact person's telephone number

Figure 4.5. Event Content Type

Published events will have links to .ical and .vcal files which can be added to calendar or appointment applications.

The Event Start and Event End fields are the only required fields among these.

Plone specifically evaluates the additional entry-fields in order to offer simple event management services:

- The structured entries are displayed in a table in the view display of each Event.

- The "Events" tab on the main navigation bar contains a list of the most recent events.

- The "Events" portlet lists each of the next five coming events. For each event, you will see a title, place, and beginning date. If you hold the mouse cursor over the title, the beginning lines of the event's description will appear.

- Plone enters Events into the Calendar portlet. The title of the portlet informs you as to which month is currently displayed. It also contains links to the preceding and following months; the current month is displayed by default. The current day is highlighted with an orange frame. Days for which at least one Event has been planned are highlighted in the calendar and serve as links to a list which contains all events taking place on that day. You will also see any Events planned for a given day, listed with starting and ending times, and titles, when holding the mouse cursor over the date.

- If you would also like your computer's calendar to record the event, you can download calendar files in iCal- and vCal-formats (iCalendar/vCalendar) in the view display among the item actions for an Event.

The Events overview list and portlet only recognize Events which have received a "Published" workflow state.

Plone checks to make sure that your date entries for the beginning and end of an Event are valid, and that the start date does not lie after the end date.

Images

The "Image" item type is used for site images. It is normally not necessary to use the Add New action to add an Image. Usually your content item will already have an upload form or you can use the Insert/Edit image in TinyMCE to add an image to a content item. A few things to remember:

- If you are viewing the contents of a folder, Images will display in the content listing as well.

- If you added an Image to a Page using the rich-text editor, the Image will be listed in the same folder as the Page, unless otherwise specified.

- With Images (like Files) a title is *not* required. If you do not provide a title for an Image/File, Plone will use the file name for the Title and ID. This way the image or file will have the correct file extension in the URL. You can always edit it again if you need a title.

- To prevent images from appearing in portlets, the Admin user can choose to hide all images from appearing in search results and navigation portlets. If this is not enabled, you can still set the individual image so that it does not appear in navigation portlets. From the Edit Bar for the image item, choose *Settings --> Exclude from navigation*.

By default, the image content type (like the file content type) does not have any workflow states. That means that whether it is published depends on the publish-state of the folder containing it. For the most part, that usually means that images are automatically published when the folder itself is published. On the other hand, if the folder containing an image is private or unpublished, then the images inside that folder will remain private or unpublished as well.

The Image content type has a Transform action on the Edit toolbar which anyone with editing rights can use. The Transform page lets you flip or transform the image. These options are not available in the rich text editor (which only lets you resize the image).

Figure 4.6. Transforming an image content type

The Transform action lets you rotate or flip an image item.

Updating an Image appearing in multiple places

Most of the time you should not need to add or even edit an individual image item. But suppose many pages reference a specific image (say the company logo), and then the marketing department switches to a new logo; how do you do that?

The easiest way to do that is to go to the folder containing the image, choose Edit and replace the image.

Figure 4.7. Replacing an image

Image

Current image JPEG image — 15 KB

○ **Keep existing image**
○ **Replace with new image:**

Choose File No file chosen

Replacing an image allows you to switch an image which is referenced on several different pages.

Files

Like the image item type, the File item type does not have any workflow state. That means its workflow state depends on the state of the Folder containing it. If the Folder is private, then all files inside it will be private. If the folder is public, then all Files within it will also be public. An Admin user can change this default, but generally it is common for Files to have no workflow state.

A File item type is a generic type. It has the same properties as pages except that instead of a text field, there is a file upload field which allows you to choose a file for upload. With the help of a file item, you can publish and offer any desired file for download on your website. The type, inner structure, and format of the file are not subject to any limits.

The disadvantage with files is that Plone is only able to recognize a small number of them and, because it has no knowledge about the structure and format of other files, is not able to see into them. Because of this, full-text searches will only function with PDF, Office, and simple text files but not with any other formats. For this reason, you should always save texts as "Page" or "News" items and images as "Image" items if possible, even though it is technically possible to save them as "File" items.

Along with the title and description field, the view display of a File item also contains the name of the file, and a link for downloading it, as well as particulars about the file's size and MIME type.

An exception to this is with text files such as plain text, source code from programs, or HTML text. In these cases, Plone is able to display the content of the files. It recognizes text documents because their MIME type begins with "text/". Normally, your browser ensures that the appropriate MIME type is sent along with a file upon uploading.

Depending on the type of file and the configuration settings for your web browser, Files are either opened in your browser with the help of an appropriate program, or saved onto your computer. In many cases, both options are available; the web browser asks you what you would like to do with the file.

Similar to images, when you select the Edit option for a file, you are presented with a upload form to browse and upload the file from your local computer. Here are some things to keep in mind:

- When you upload a file, it will retain its original name and extension within the File item, even though you will manually need to specify a name.

- If Plone recognizes the file type (.doc, .pdf, etc.), it will put the appropriate icon beside it in the folder view.

- A title is not required for Files. If you do not provide a title for a file, Plone will use the file name for the Title and ID. This way the image or file will have the correct file extension in the URL. You can always edit it again if you need a title.

- It is highly recommended to add a description and possibly even a tag to a file you uploaded. Remember that Plone may not be able to read the content contained within a file. The only way that a visitor might be able to find this file is through the metadata you provide.

- Depending on your web server, there may be a maximum file size allowed for uploading. Remember, if your file is empty, the system will not allow it to be uploaded.

- The Admin user can allow File items to be versioned. (That means that every time you upload an updated version of the Excel spreadsheet, Plone will keep all earlier versions of it). There are two caveats to this:

  1. By default versioning is turned off for the file type. This is done to prevent several versions of binary files from burdening the Zope database. The Admin user will need to turn versioning on.

2. If versioning is turned on, you will be able to see the History of the file but not be able to use Plone to compare two different uploads. You will need to compare them manually or use a third party tool to do that.

If you need to update a File, you can simply go to the Folder containing the File and select the File. Instead of downloading the file, you will see a URL with the item's description and a download URL.

- When you navigate to the **Contents** view of a folder which contains files, you can move/copy/paste/delete/change the state of multiple files at once.

Figure 4.8. How files appear in the Contents view of a folder

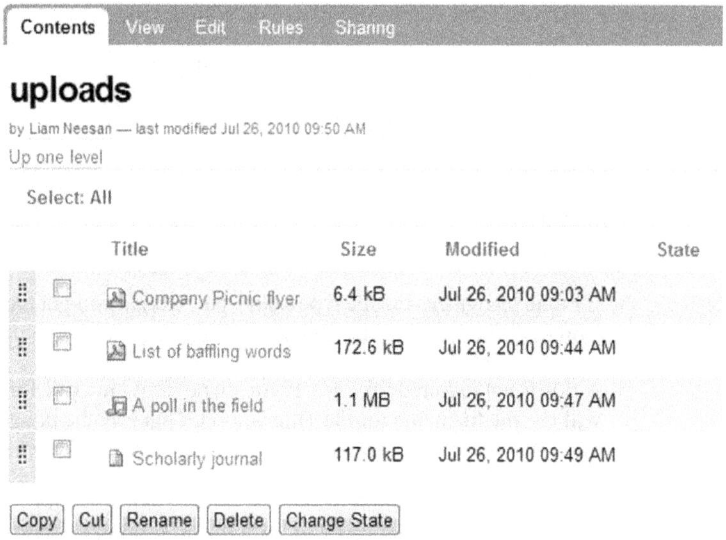

Familiar icons identify the type of file in a folder.

Names and URLs for a File

It can be confusing to figure out what URL to give people for a file you uploaded. Part of the problem is that the URL doesn't usually end with the file extension of the file itself. For a company picnic flyer, you might see these URLs:

- **http://www.pendelton.edu/academics/physics/dick-solomon-stuff/pdfs/company-picnic-flyer** Clicking on this link will open the PDF from your browser.

- **http://www.pendelton.edu/academics/physics/dick-solomon-stuff/pd-fs/company-picnic-flyer/at_download/file** Clicking this URL will also open the same PDF from your browser.

- **http://pendelton.edu/academics/physics/dick-solomon-stuff/pdfs/com-pany-picnic-flyer/view** This will not open the PDF from your browser but direct you to a page containing a single link to the PDF. For users with editing rights, they can edit the file information or upload a new version of it.

Using TinyMCE to upload things

Even though it is possible to add an image or a file by using the Add New drop-down menu, you can also perform these actions from within the TinyMCE editor. In fact it is probably easier to do it this way. See the section called "Adding Images and Files from TinyMCE " [47].

Other Ways to Upload Files

Plone 4 supports BLOBs (Binary Large Objects). Previously, it was not easy for Plone to handle the uploading of large files; it was also cumbersome because whenever large files were uploaded, the overall database size increased. The new support for BLOBs lets Plone store larger files separately from the Zope database, thus improving performance and administration.

So far this improvement is not really visible to end users, but it now makes it easier for Plone developers to create add-ons to facilitate the easy uploading of larger multimedia files.

It also might be possible to use third party tools to upload larger files to a Plone site. For example Plone's support for the WEBDAV protocol lets a user upload a gigantic file to a folder through a WEBDAV tool instead of a browser.

Keeping files in a separate folder?

If many users need to upload many files on a regular basis, it may be a good idea to create a common folder to put them in. In this case, the common folder would be named 'Uploads' or 'PDFs' or 'MP3s' or something equally appropriate. This is more of a housekeeping issue, but keeping a common folder for uploads can make it much easier for people to find your files and link to them using the Insert/Edit Link dialog. It can also make it easier to administer actions on multiple items simultaneously, instead of one at a time.

It is theoretically possible for an Admin user to create a Content Rule to move Files with a certain extension (like .PDF) to a single folder. See Chapter 9, *Using*

Content Rules [142] for more information. An alternative to creating content rules is creating a Collection which lists files with a certain extension. The URL for that Collection could list all the PDFs uploaded to the site, or could be customized even further. Collections will be covered in greater detail in the next chapter.

Links

On a Plone website, you can manage links to other websites as easily as any other types of content. The "Link" item type exists for doing this, and the link's content simply consists of an Internet address. In the view display of a link item, you will find a title, a description of the resource, and a link to the address.

The link content type was important in earlier versions of Plone when it was not as easy to add hyperlinks within the rich text editor. However, TinyMCE has improved things considerably, and it is generally unnecessary to use this content type any more. (In fact, it may be wise to hide the type from users, so they don't become confused).

There are cases where the link content type is still used. For example, one site asked users to use the link content type to store URLS for YouTube videos. If users wanted to embed one of these YouTube videos into a page, the user would simply choose the Insert/Edit Link button on TinyMCE and find the link to the YouTube video that was stored on the Plone site. Other site planners might dream up other anticipated uses for this content type.

If you have a reason to use the link content type, make sure to type a meaningful summary of what is found at this link. Links nowadays may be dynamically generated and meaningless to the site visitor unless you describe the title or author of the link as well.

Chapter 5. Folder and Collection Item Types

In the previous chapter, we covered simple content types, and the properties and behaviors common to all default content types.

In this chapter, we will look at two content types which are slightly more complex: folders and collections. These are "container content" types—content types which contain other content types.

General Properties and Behavior

Although folders and collections have distinct features, it is important to remember that they share many of the configurable properties described in the section called "The Edit display" [60]. These properties include: publishing dates, tags, summaries, contributor information, whether to allow comments, or whether to exclude comments from navigation. Each of these properties is described more fully in the previous chapter.

Folder content type

The basic concept of the folder is simple, but folders can be tricky to use unless you understand a few things first:

1. Folders are used to organize and group your content.

2. Folders should contain similar kinds of content. You can restrict what kinds of content can be added to a folder.

3. To add a content item, you will usually need to be at the URL for a folder.

4. Plone folders don't really exist on the web server. They are all stored inside the Zope database.

5. There are several ways you can configure the default view of a folder.

6. It's easy to move/copy/delete/change the state of multiple items in a folder.

7. Folders have security settings and can be shared. If you set a security setting on the sharing tab, it will apply to all items inside a folder.

8. If a folder is unpublished or private, published items inside the folder will still be visible (generally). This can sometimes cause confusion because if users try to go up one level, they will see an error message.

9. You can manually change the order of how items appear by going to the Contents tab and moving individual items up and down with your mouse.

The Folder Metaphor

With Plone, a folder can contain a folder (i.e., a subfolder) or a file, a page or other content items. Before scripting languages like php were used to create dynamic web pages, the directory structures for URLs would roughly correspond to the actual files and folders on the web server. For the URL **www.pendelton.edu/news/press-releases/**, you usually could find a root directory with a news folder and inside that was another folder called press-releases. For static sites, that still is the case, but now most content management systems use scripts to manipulate the final URL. On a blog-based content management system, the URL may look like this:
http://thirdrock.blogs.newspaper.com/2010/02/05/teamx-interplanetary-report/

If you looked at the web server's file system, you would not see a directory called 2010 or a subdirectory called 02. That is because the content management system is manipulating the URL to make it easier to read and type. Plone does something similar. For the URL
http://physics.pendelton.edu/student-life/intramurals

you won't be able to find a student-life directory or a directory called *intramurals* on the web server file structure. In fact, most (if not all) of the data resides in the Zope database (ZODB). Plone preserves this metaphor of folders for website content. Most users will be able to create a folder for new content and put items into this folder. It was a conscious design decision by Plone developers to allow users to think of content in terms of folders and files (Other content management systems like Drupal and WordPress specifically do not do this).

Using Folders to Organize and Group Content

The main use of folders is to organize your content. If you are a college, it would make sense to have an Academics folder. Under that, you would expect to have a set of subfolders for academic departments (anthropology, physics, etc.) Inside the physics department subfolder, for example, you could expect to have separate folders for each faculty member or perhaps for each research project within the department. Obviously, the content for these folders can often overlap, but in cases where content is discrete from one another, it makes sense to create folders. Keep in mind that you should not have too many levels of folders, or you may end up making your content difficult to find.

In Chapter 11, *Improving Navigation & Findability* [173] , we will cover practical tips for organizing your content into folders. For now, it suffices to say that folders should not be the only way to organize content. (Tags, Portlets, and Collections can also aid in this).

Folders are where you add content!

As stated in the previous chapter, you can only add content inside a folder. For that reason, you need to be able to know the difference between being on a URL for a folder and being on a URL for another content type. Here are some ways to tell whether you are currently at a folder:

- In a folder you generally see a list of items which are inside that folder. The appearance of the list may vary (as will be described below), and in some cases the Admin user may customize the folder to show a page instead of a list of items, but having a list of items appear is a good sign you are at a folder.

- Assuming that you have full rights over the folder, you will see at least two tabs on the action toolbar: **Contents** and **Add New**.

- Folder names will appear in the breadcrumbs link that appears as a navigational aid at the top.

Figure 5.1. Breadcrumbs for Navigation

We are currently in a folder called "Dick Solomon stuff." The breadcrumbs show the series of folders which are above the current one. (Physics is the one immediately above).

Restricting what content can be added in folders

As a content creator, you may not have the rights to control which item types can be added to a folder. However if you are the owner of the folder (or are an Admin user), you will see an additional option on the Add New drop-down: **Restrictions**. After choosing that, you will see three options:

- Use parent folder settings.

- User portal default

- Select manually.

If you select the option **Select Manually**, more options will become visible.

Figure 5.2. Restricting addable content types

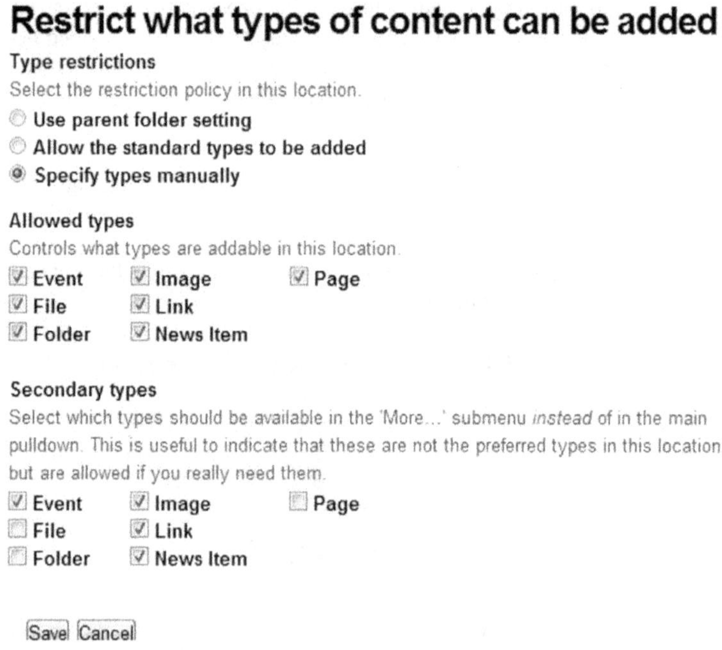

Restrict what types of content can be added

Type restrictions
Select the restriction policy in this location.
○ Use parent folder setting
○ Allow the standard types to be added
◉ Specify types manually

Allowed types
Controls what types are addable in this location.
☑ Event   ☑ Image   ☑ Page
☑ File   ☑ Link
☑ Folder ☑ News Item

Secondary types
Select which types should be available in the 'More...' submenu *instead* of in the main pulldown. This is useful to indicate that these are not the preferred types in this location, but are allowed if you really need them.
☑ Event   ☑ Image   ☐ Page
☐ File   ☑ Link
☐ Folder ☑ News Item

Save Cancel

Items which you check under Secondary types will be hidden from the Add Menu, but can still be added.

In the above screenshot, we wanted to limit what kinds of content can be added. To do this, all hidden items under the "More..." submenu would be selected as Secondary types as well as Allowed types. If a type is selected as both Allowed and Secondary, the Secondary classification will take precedence. Types not selected as Allowed cannot be specified as Secondary. In this example all the types are still addable, but the default drop-down list will look like this:

Figure 5.3. Add New Items menu (when restricted)

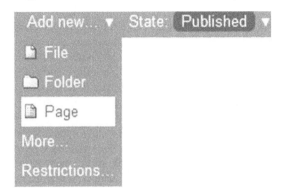

The More option will let you add all the hidden content types

Setting the default appearance for a folder

Here's where it can get slightly confusing. You can set how the Folder is displayed by choosing the **Display** action on the top right section of the edit toolbar. Underneath that, you have:

- Summary content

- All content

- Tabular view

- Thumbnail view

- Select a content item as default view.

- (A custom view added by the site developer or administrator).

Rearranging items in your folder is easy!

It is essential that the listing of content items in a Folder is logical, intuitive, and usable for the user. In addition to providing many different displays for Folders, Plone also lets you manually arrange Folder items in any order you want. Simply go to the Contents tab of your Folder, and grab the left side of each item and "lift" an item to where you want to put it. This is helpful if you want to call attention to certain items over others. Also, if your Folder contains different content items (some of which are not relevant to what the visitor will be seeking), you can simply move the item(s) to the bottom of the stack. This method of manually arranging content items might become impractical if your Folder contains too many items, but it should be fairly manageable if your folder contains less than 20 items.

Suppose you want to exclude the Image content type from showing in your folder view and automatically arrange the items in a folder by last modification date. To do that, simply add a Collection item to your folder and set criteria in the collection. In this example, you will add 3 criteria: 1) Show all content items except images, 2) Select location to be the parent folder; and 3) Set Sort Order by Modification Date. *Note:* you will need to have the right to add a collection to a folder and to publish it before you can configure one.

In the early days of Plone, the views for a folder were fairly simple. On the next figure, you can see the **Tabular View**.

Figure 5.4. Tabular view of a Folder

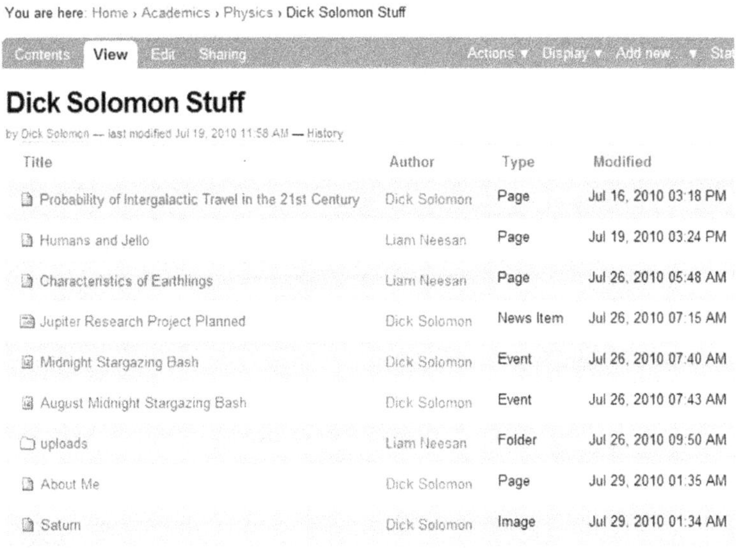

You are here: Home › Academics › Physics › Dick Solomon Stuff

| Contents | **View** | Edit | Sharing | | | Actions ▼ | Display ▼ | Add new ▼ | Sta |

Dick Solomon Stuff

by Dick Solomon — last modified Jul 19, 2010 11:58 AM — History

Title	Author	Type	Modified
Probability of Intergalactic Travel in the 21st Century	Dick Solomon	Page	Jul 16, 2010 03:18 PM
Humans and Jello	Liam Neesan	Page	Jul 19, 2010 03:24 PM
Characteristics of Earthlings	Liam Neesan	Page	Jul 26, 2010 05:48 AM
Jupiter Research Project Planned	Dick Solomon	News Item	Jul 26, 2010 07:15 AM
Midnight Stargazing Bash	Dick Solomon	Event	Jul 26, 2010 07:40 AM
August Midnight Stargazing Bash	Dick Solomon	Event	Jul 26, 2010 07:43 AM
uploads	Liam Neesan	Folder	Jul 26, 2010 09:50 AM
About Me	Dick Solomon	Page	Jul 29, 2010 01:35 AM
Saturn	Dick Solomon	Image	Jul 29, 2010 01:34 AM

Tabular view shows a lot of metadata, but isn't user-friendly.

The view which is used most frequently is the **Standard View**. It includes the title, creator name, modified data and the description. It is a compact way for displaying information.

Figure 5.5. Standard view of a folder

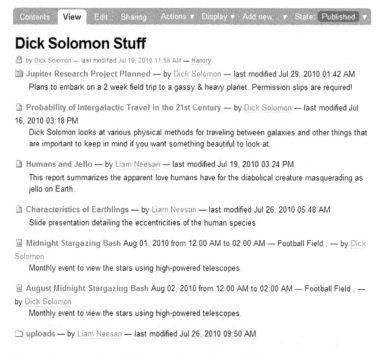

The standard folder view is informative but a little overwhelming.

You also had the summary view which was closer to a typical landing page on a web site.

Figure 5.6. Summary view of a folder

Dick Solomon Stuff

by Dick Solomon — last modified Jul 19, 2010 11:58 AM — History

Jupiter Research Project Planned

by Dick Solomon — last modified Jul 29, 2010 01:42 AM

Plans to embark on a 2 week field trip to a gassy & heavy planet. Permission
slips are required!

Read More...

Probability of Intergalactic Travel in the 21st Century

Dick Solomon looks at various physical methods for traveling between galaxies and other things that are
important to keep in mind if you want something beautiful to look at.

Read More...

Humans and Jello

This report summarizes the apparent love humans have for the diabolical creature masquerading as jello
on Earth.

Read More...

Characteristics of Earthlings

Slide presentation detailing the eccentricities of the human species

The summary view lists the title, summary and any accompanying graphic. It is easier to read.

Another option is **Thumbnail View**. This shows the standard view, except that
thumbnail images of Images inside the Folder will be shown at the top. This view
is primarily useful when your folder primarily contains images and you wish to
let people view it as a gallery. It is less useful in cases where the folder contains
different content types. In the illustration below, one Image is directly inside the
Folder. The second Image is actually representing a subfolder (called **uploads**)
containing that image.

Figure 5.7. Thumbnail view of a folder

You are here: Home › Academics › Physics › Dick Solomon Stuff

Contents | **View** | Edit | Sharing | Actions ▼ | Display ▼ | Add new... ▼ | State: Published ▼

Dick Solomon Stuff

by Dick Solomon — last modified Jul 19, 2010 11:58 AM — History

Saturn

uploads (2)

Jupiter Research Project Planned — by Dick Solomon — last modified Jul 29, 2010 01:42 AM
   Plans to embark on a 2 week field trip to a gassy & heavy planet. Permission slips are required!

Probability of Intergalactic Travel in the 21st Century — by Dick Solomon — last modified Jul 16, 2010 03:18 PM
   Dick Solomon looks at various physical methods for traveling between galaxies and other things that are important to keep in mind if you want something beautiful to look at.

Humans and Jello — by Liam Neesan — last modified Jul 19, 2010 03:24 PM
   This report summarizes the apparent love humans have for the diabolical creature masquerading as jello on Earth.

Characteristics of Earthlings — by Liam Neesan — last modified Jul 26, 2010 05:48 AM
   Slide presentation detailing the eccentricities of the human species

Midnight Stargazing Bash Aug 01, 2010 from 12:00 AM to 02:00 AM — Football Field , — by Dick Solomon
   Monthly event to view the stars using high-powered telescopes.

Thumbnail view is used mainly if the folder contains only images and you wish to allow the visitor to view it like a gallery.

The **All Content** display just dumps all content from every item onto a single URL. This view can sometimes look messy, but is useful if the Folder will mainly contain lots of Pages (and ideally text-only pages) that are only a few paragraphs long. For example, you could keep a daily journal of observations, with one Page per day. Or various people could contribute their thoughts on a particular topic (i.e., "What do you believe is true even though you cannot prove it?"), and an All Content view could display all the thoughts on a single URL .

Figure 5.8. The All Content view of a folder

The All Content view is highly readable and works best when the folder contains several pages which are short and not full of images.

One downside of the All Content view is that it will show different content types on the same view (That means images, events, files, etc.), so if your Folder contains too many different content types, it can look "messy" or even unreadable. One way around that is to go to the **Contents** view of your folder and manually move weird content to the bottom of the list. You aren't exactly hiding this content but making it less prominent in the folder display.

One final downside is that there is no automatic mechanism to limit the number of content items which are fully shown for this URL.

Despite these caveats, All Content can definitely be useful in certain situations.

Using a default page instead of a folder display

One more option exists for how to display a folder. You can set a default page for the folder which will appear when a visitor has reached the folder URL.

To select a default page, choose the option **Select content item as default view** on the **Display** tab. At this point, a pop-up dialog will appear which lets you choose an item:

Figure 5.9. Selecting a content item as default folder view

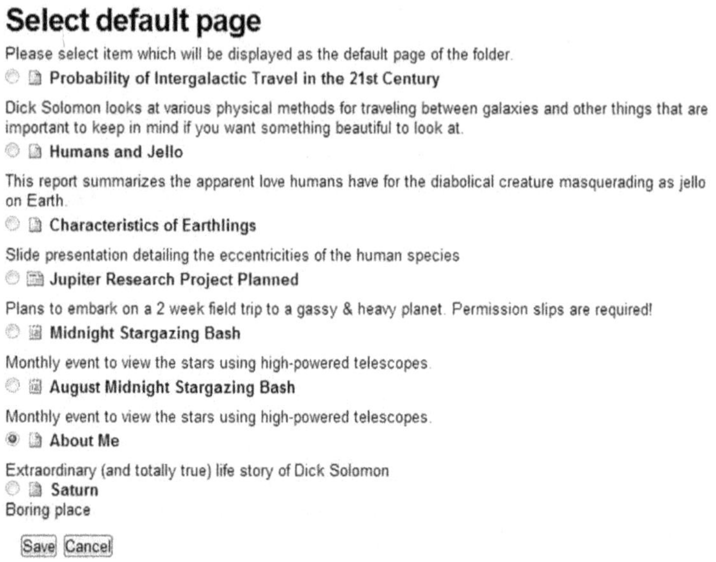

Select default page

Please select item which will be displayed as the default page of the folder.

○ 🗋 Probability of Intergalactic Travel in the 21st Century

Dick Solomon looks at various physical methods for traveling between galaxies and other things that are important to keep in mind if you want something beautiful to look at.

○ 🗋 Humans and Jello

This report summarizes the apparent love humans have for the diabolical creature masquerading as jello on Earth.

○ 🗋 Characteristics of Earthlings

Slide presentation detailing the eccentricities of the human species

○ 🗐 Jupiter Research Project Planned

Plans to embark on a 2 week field trip to a gassy & heavy planet. Permission slips are required!

○ 🗐 Midnight Stargazing Bash

Monthly event to view the stars using high-powered telescopes.

○ 🗐 August Midnight Stargazing Bash

Monthly event to view the stars using high-powered telescopes.

◉ 🗋 About Me

Extraordinary (and totally true) life story of Dick Solomon

○ 🗋 Saturn

Boring place

[Save] [Cancel]

Clicking the Display tab on the action bar will let you choose a content item to be the default view.

Here are some things to keep in mind when using an item as a default page:

1. By setting a default page, you prevent site visitors from having a way to view content items of a Folder as a list. This can be good or bad. When you use default pages, you are committing to manually updating this page as needed. This actually isn't as much of a bother as it sounds. Suppose the physics department wants its department page to be a default view of a Folder. This allows the department to choose which links are visible and to use images and page styles to lay everything out.

2. URLs become confusing. That means the Folder URL and the page item URL will have exactly the same content.

Figure 5.10. 3 Ways to spot the difference between a page and a folder item with a default page view

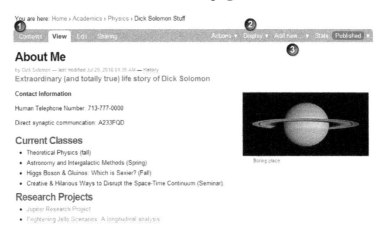

1) Contents tab will be visible. 2)Display tab will be visible. 3)Add New drop-down menu will be shown.

3. If a Folder is private, the default page can still be published and viewable. Although that is consistent with Plone's workflow rules, it may seem counterintuitive to content creators who don't worry about workflow details.

4. When editing, you sometimes forget if you are editing the page itself or the Folder. For this reason, Plone includes a reminder at the top of the page.

Figure 5.11. Message when editing default Page

If you see this message, you know you are viewing a page which has been chosen as the default view for a Folder.

5. If you set an item to be the default view of the Container, you need to be extra careful that all published content inside that Folder is accessible in some way. After you set an item to be a default view, you are effectively preventing the visitor from seeing a list of all published content inside that folder. That might very well be your intent. But you may need to manually add Links or Portlets or Collections to allow users to see other items.

For this reason Plone usability guru Joel Burton has described default pages as problematic because they blur the distinction between Folders and Pages. As an alternative, Burton recommends that site developers create a custom content folder type which is the same as the regular folder but with an extra field for editing text. That means you'd have two identical folder types: the default folder type (when you want it to list all items in the folder) and a custom folder type whose view you can edit just like a Page. Although this method requires some customization, it is an elegant way to mitigate user confusion.

Rearranging the default order of items in a folder view

One common complaint about Folders is that their listing appears to be in an arbitrary order. While this is true, if you go to the **Contents** tab when in a folder, you can easily change the order in which items appear in your folder.

After you have selected the Contents tab of a Folder, the items will be listed as rows of alternating color. If you move your cursor above the "handle" on the left side of the row, you will be able to "lift" the item and move it higher or lower within the folder.

Figure 5.12. Arranging the order of items in a Folder

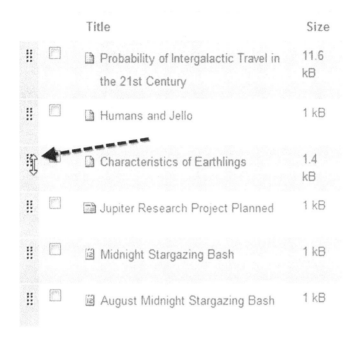

When the cursor changes to an up-and-down arrow, you can lift the row and move it up or down to change its order in the listing.

Performing Actions on Multiple items in a folder

The Contents tab on a folder lets you perform actions on multiple items within the same Folder at once. Simply check all the items you want and choose a button corresponding to the operation you wish to perform. Here are actions you can perform on multiple items from the content tab of a Folder:

- Copy

- Cut

- Rename

- Paste

- Delete

- Change State

Rename and Delete are self-explanatory. Change State lets you change the publication state of multiple items simultaneously. This is helpful if you want to coordinate the publication of several items so that they all happen at once. Although you can decide to change the state of multiple items in different workflow states, the resulting state must be the same for all items you are changing.

Moving/copying/pasting items into a different folder

One unique feature about Plone is that it lets you move one or more items to different locations on a site. This can help not only to organize your site better, it also lets you make templates which you can clone to different parts of your site.

Let us suppose that all academic departments tend to have similar (if not identical) pages. An academic department page might use these templates:

- a telephone directory for staff members

- a sample biographical page for faculty members.

- A description of the college major for that department

- Map & Directions for the department office

- standard logos and graphics

- student work-study page

Generally every academic department will have these kinds of pages. Rather than having each department create their own version of these items from scratch, you can store these templates in a folder and then copy them into every department folder. You can also leave them permanently in a private state, so the templates themselves will not be visible to anonymous visitors. In fact, if you are adding a new folder for a department that you need to add frequently, you can simply store the template items inside a folder and copy the entire folder to where you need it. The point here is not to discourage content creator from creating pages from scratch but to save time in composing standard pages. If you find that you are having to clone a certain item a lot, that may suggest a need for the site developers to create a custom content type which is addable from the Add New drop-down list.

Although in this context we are talking about performing these actions from the Content tab of a Folder, actions like move/ copy/ paste are available to use on the content bar for individual items. You don't need to be in a folder to cut/copy/paste something; you only need to be able to have edit rights to a content item. If you have editing rights, the **Actions** tab will appear on the right side above the content item.

The Admin user can use the move/copy/paste action for content rules. For example, suppose you want all department events to be moved to an events folder at the root of the site. You can create a content rule that will move all events to a certain folder after they have published. (The same effect can be achieved by creating a collection in the target folder which will dynamically list all event items which have been published in various departments).

> Caution: If you have added links via the *Related Items* field for an item, these links will **not** be transferred when you move or copy content. You may need to add them again manually after moving.

Collections

A Collection is a more advanced content type which is normally created and edited only by users with the Admin role.

Collections allow you to create and display a filtered and sorted list of content items using one or more criteria. Even though a collection appears on a single URL and may include introductory or boilerplate information at the top or bottom, it is essentially a stored query of content items. In Plone-speak, a collection is a separate content type which shares some general characteristics of all content types (such as metadata). Like folders, a collection can contain other content items, but these content items are automatically added and displayed; the user does not add individual items to a collection; the collection merely displays published items which meet some criteria.

The best thing about a collection is that it applies not only to existing content but also future content. It arose from the need in most content management systems to have a better way to organize links to content. Landing pages which simply link to existing content can be constructed manually, but this takes time to create and requires constant updating. Dynamically generated landing pages can contain lots of links, but it may be presented or ordered in a way not useful for site visitors. Collections solve that problem by letting you fine tune how the landing page appears and what links appear on this URL (and in what order).

Collections can perform a variety of functions on a site:

- Every collection can includes its own RSS feed, so if you need a reason to generate an RSS feed, just create a collection of the items and voilà! You have made an RSS feed that will update continuously.

- Collections let you exclude one or more content types from an list of items. For example, in many cases you don't want images to appear on a folder's list of items.

- Collections can consolidate items from different folders on the site so that they are listed in one central location. That essentially means that you can display relevant content items regardless of where they were originally added.

- Collections allow you to reuse a search query while offering a stable and human-friendly URL.

- You can use collections to show the order in which items are scheduled to be published.

- Collections can be used for portlets that are more fine-tuned than the default portlet types.

- Collections can be used as default content items to display when viewing a folder. Because collections include a text field, that allows you to add a preface to a dynamically generated list of items. (You could even include images or logos at the top).

- Collections can allow for a "sideways" method of viewing the contents of a folder. If a folder already contains a large amount of items, a collection can provide an alternate way of showing a subset of a folder's content.

- Collections allows site visitors to discover new items.

Most content creators don't need to worry about Collections except to realize that some site URLs may not be Pages but non-editable Collections consisting of content from different locations on the site. Except for the boilerplate text at the top and bottom of the URL, the list of items on these Collections require that a user have the right permissions. It is not a power that content creators will normally have. However, Admins usually put Collections around the site in order to make information easier to find. Probably the most important thing to remember is that Collections are easy to customize. Suppose an Admin user created a Collection page consisting of an alphabetical listing of the faculty home pages. It would be a relatively trivial matter to edit the Collection so that it lists all faculty pages except for faculty members from the medical school. If you see that a Collection page is becoming unwieldy, you can ask for the original Collection to be modified so that the Collection page is more usable.

Obtaining rights to make a Collection

The ability to add or edit Collections requires privileges beyond what the normal user would have. The Admin user has the ability to add and edit Collections which applies globally. Creating a Collection implies that the user has access to all site content, and that would not be true for a typical user.

Who can view Collection results?

You can add a Collection into a specific folder, but a Collection when published will potentially grab links to content from anywhere on the site. That is why it is important to specify criteria so that your Collection displays only the content you wish to display and nothing more.

You may notice that when you are editing a criteria (and viewing potential results) that content items will have a different color (i.e., private/unpublished items will be displayed in **red** font, pending items will be displayed in **orange** font; published items will appear generally in **blue** font). In fact, these colors will only appear to Admins; these colors will generally not appear to site visitors or logged in users because users generally can only see published items and items which they created themselves. (The Admin user controls this by configuring the item's workflow of the item. This is explained in more detail in Chapter 8, *Collaborative Editing: Workflows* [129]).

When configuring a Collection, you can specify that the *Review State* be only **Published**. For safety's sake, you might want every Collection to include this criteria; on the other hand, Plone workflow defaults are generally sane – so most of the time you don't need to worry. If there is a visibility problem, it generally is because a user or group of users has received overly generous viewing rights (i.e. the *Can View* column is checked for that item or containing folder).

To summarize: Even though the Admin user might see some private and pending content items in Collection results, ordinary users won't normally see these things (aside from their own content). Configuring a Collection won't cause private or pending content to be visible to the wrong people.

Adding a Collection

Plone 4.2 did a facelift on the interface for configuring Collections. It is more user-friendly. The preview feature lets you see instantly how your choice of search term will affect the results.

Here are the major steps for creating Collections:

1. Decide where you want to put your Collection. You will need to choose which folder should contain the Collection.

2. Set search terms and sort order for Collection results.

3. Configure how results appear and add introductory text (if needed).

4. Test the results when logged on as a user who is not an Admin.

The Collection will display at a single URL, so you need to navigate to the Plone folder corresponding to it. Then you add a Collection as you would add any other content item: (by choosing the **Add New** drop-down menu on the right side). Regardless of where you put your Collection, this Collection will generally have the ability to display content items from all over the site. The only way you can override this is to add a **location** criterion to your search term. (This will be discussed below).

Configuring search terms for a Collection

After you have completed the title & description for a Collection, you will see a drop-down menu under the **Search Term** You will configure one or more search terms (also called "criteria") to control what results are displayed from your Collection. Initially, there is only a single row. But whenever you start configuring that row, a new row will automatically appear underneath. If you click the Search Term drop-down menu, a lot of options will appear:

- **Dates**: Event start date, Expiration Date, Event End Date, Effective Date, Creation Date, Modification Date

- **Text**: Description, Title, Searchable Text, Tag

- **Metadata**: Creator, Location, Review State, Short Name (id), Type

Whenever you choose a search term, you will notice that the two drop-down boxes beside it will dynamically change as well. For example, if you select **Tag**, then the second box will say "Is" and the third box will be a drop-down checklist containing all available choices.

The third drop-down box will allow you to choose more than one thing or to type more than one word in it.

At the far right of the Search Terms boxes there will be a listing of how many items satisfy this search term. In this way, you can see in real time how many items survive this narrowing of the search.

For now, we will skip the search terms under Dates and start with Metadata and then Text. Finally we will cover Dates.

Metadata Search Terms

Usually a Collection will contain at least one metadata option. The options available are: Creator, Location, Review State, Short Name (id), Type.

Type. This is probably the most important search term to configure. Generally, all Collections should include a search term for type. If you fail to do this, the Collection may display too many unwanted things (i.e., image files, PDFs, etc.) You can check more than one type if appropriate.

Review State. As stated earlier, Plone security defaults are sane enough that you don't normally need to add this search term to your Collection. But if you are using a custom workflow or are particularly paranoid about letting some users not see pending or private items, you can specify something here. Generally though, it's not needed.

Short Name (id). Here you are searching for the slug that comprises the item's URL (i.e., , not the human-friendly title) for the item. In the example listed below, a user may have created a folder named "Press Releases", but the way it appears in the URL uses all lowercase letters and hyphens between individual words (i.e., *press-releases*). Therefore the short name (id) would be "press-releases" instead of "Press Releases."

Creator. In the third box, you will *not* be presented with a list of users, but must manually type the user's account name for the search term to work. The search term you must use here is the login ID (i.e., *dsolomon*) not the human readable name (i.e., *Dick Solomon*). You must spell a complete word before any search results will start to appear. If you want to find the user ID of the creator, simply go to the item itself, click on the **Creators** tab, and then note who is listed on the **Creators** text field (usually this value is added automatically here).

Path. The location of an item in the site. The second box presents two options: *Relative Path* and *Absolute Path*. Here are some examples of values you would use for each case. Suppose your website had these URLs:

- *www.pendeltonstate.edu/dept/physics/my-collection* (what you are currently configuring)

- *www.pendeltonstate.edu/dept/physics/classlectures/*

- *www.pendeltonstate.edu/dept/press-releases/*

- *www.pendeltonstate.edu/sports/*

Here is how you would configure a path using relative and absolute syntax.

Table 5.1. Using Absolute and Relative Paths in Collection Search Terms

Intended path	Relative	Absolute
Choose any item which lives in the parent folder and all folders below the parent folder.	../	/dept/physics
Choose any item which lives in the great-grandparent folder and all folders below the great-grandparent folder.	../../../	/ (i.e., this is the root level)
Choose any item which lives in the pressreleases folder which is inside the parent's folder.	../../press-releases/	/dept/press-releases/
In the child folder called pressreleases, choose all items.	classlectures/	/dept /physics/ classlectures
Choose any item which lives inside the sports folder which is both in the great-grandparent folder and inside the top folder.	../../../sports	/sports/

For both relative and absolute paths, it is optional and unnecessary to include another slash at the end. Thus, **/dept/pressreleases/** and **/dept/pressreleases** mean the same thing. On the other hand, when typing an absolute path, the first thing you type must be a slash, or the search term will not be accurately processed. If you type nothing but a "/" for an absolute path, that means the Collection will include results from the entire site. (That is the default – unless otherwise specified).

An important limitation of using path as a search term is that Collections work recursively on all pages and subfolders inside a certain folder. That means you cannot hide results in one of the subfolders from appearing in Collection results.

Text Search Terms in a Collection

The options listed in the Search Terms drop-down menu under Text are fairly straightforward. The **tags** option is probably the easiest to configure because the third box presents you with a checklist of all available tags. All you need to do is to check one or more tags and view the results. But that works only when content creators have been giving tags to content items. You can't necessarily assume that users are doing this reliably and consistently.

For text fields, you can type the usual search parameters to narrow search results. Here are some basic guidelines:

- If using multiple words, it is not necessary to put them inside quotation marks.

- Words are not case sensitive.

- Generally Plone searches only for complete words. For example, if you want to search for articles containing the word "basketball", when you start typing "basket," no results will appear until you spell out the complete word "basketball."

- If you want your Collection query to locate both items containing the word "Africa" and "African", you should type **Africa***.

- Both "Basketball Scores" and "Basketball + Scores" (if you type them without quotations) will show the same results. Similarly, typing "Baseball or basketball" will display items which contain either the words 'baseball' or 'basketball.'

Date Search Terms in a Collection

The final group of search terms deal with dates and events. The main challenge is knowing what exactly each date search term refers to:

- **Event Start Date** and **Event End Date** refer to date values of the event content type.

- **Effective Date** refers to when the content item was published. Most of the time you will be using this for date-oriented Collections.

- **Creation Date** refers to when the content was created (even when it was still in a private state).

- **Modification Date** refers to when the content item was last changed. In Collections, this might be misleading. Suppose you want a Collection to contain the 10 most recently published pages. What if you just now corrected a typo on a content item which was published 3 years ago? You would not normally want this item to be listed as a recent item.

- **Expiration Date** is an optional value that the content creator or editor can configure for the content item. It is used only when you want an item to disappear after a certain date (for time-sensitive material for example).

Often when you configure these kinds of search terms, you will use a predicate in the middle drop-down box to specify a relative date (i.e., *Before Today*) or a specific date by adding an integer (i.e., *Within Next ____ days*) or by finding it on a calendar pop-up (i.e., *Before Date*).

Figure 5.13. Configuring a date search term

Clicking the third box on a Date Search Term with an After Date or Before Date predicate will cause a calendar widget to appear.

Configuring how Collection results appear

The edit page for a Collection also lets you configure basic things related to how it displays on a web page.

Sort Order. Underneath the Search Term boxes is a box labeled **Sort On** with several drop-down options which roughly correspond to the drop-down options for Search Terms. Here are two things worth knowing about that:

- What you use for sorting doesn't have to be the same as what you used for Search Terms. For example, suppose you created a search criteria to show all results with the tag "Sports." You can still set the sort order by Effective Date.

- In some cases, the option you choose for sorting may be invisible in the actual search results. For example, you may choose to sort by Effective Date, but the results in the preview pane (and actual URL) will generally show only the Last Modified Date. The site developer could modify this default view, and indeed, Plone provides a way to tweak the appearance of the Collection in tabular view only. (This will be explained below).

- Checking the **Reversed Order** checkbox will cause the earliest items to appear on top and the latest at bottom. If sorting by something textual (tags, creator, title) will sort in reversed alphabetical order (Z to A).

Generally the preview pane keeps up with whatever customizations you make to the Collection. Even if the Collection normally returns 200 items, the preview will show only the top 10. It will display only 10 search results.

Body Text. You might find it strange that a content item which simply displays search results would allow you to input text as well. But the default Collection item lets you add preliminary text which is displayed between the Title and Collection search results. This lets you personalize the appearance of your search results, at least superficially. One application of this personalization is that you could add a logo or contact information. *Note:* Any content you create here will not appear in the RSS feed (and that is good really; why would you want an RSS feed to contain static unchanging content?)

Limit Search Results. The default is to display a maximum of 1000 items, but web surfers are used to results pages showing 50 or maybe 100 results on a single page. You may wish to set a lower limit if you think that this Collection could conceivably be displaying a lot of items. Keep this in mind that if you are configuring a Collection for a Collection Portlet *(See the section called "Collection Portlets" [163] for more information).*

Setting Views and Configuring Tabular View. As stated in the section called "Setting the default appearance for a folder" [82], Plone has several ways to display folder contents. A user with the right permissions can choose which display to use by selecting the appropriate option in the **Display** drop-down menu on the right toolbar. One such view is Tabular View.

Usually content creators use the **Standard View** which is also the default view. The Standard View includes the title, creator name, last modified date and a description. The Tabular View puts all items in a table. The Edit Collections interface contains several options specific to the Tabular View. You can choose which fields will appear in each column of each displayed table. Remember that these options will *only* appear in Tabular View and not for any other view and they will not appear when summoned for a Collection Portlet.

Customizing Views for a Collection

Like many other aspects of Plone, Collections may be customized by your site developer. For this reason, the Edit screen for your Collection may look different, depending on the customizations. In fact, the site developers might have actually given the content type an entirely different name.

Chapter 6. History and Checkouts

Plone allows multiple users to collaborate in writing and editing a document. Collaboration involves three steps: setting up sharing, setting up the submission/approval process, and ensuring users don't run into collaborative conflicts. This chapter will focus on how users can avoid conflicts in collaborative editing.

This chapter assumes that the content creator has rights to create and edit a content item. The next two chapters will cover the publication sequence (i.e. Workflow), and how to set up sharing.

Reverting to Previous Saves (History)

Plone has the ability to look back at previous saved versions of a content item, allowing you to compare different versions of the same content item, and even revert to an earlier version. It also lets you overview changes throughout the publication history.

If you do not see the History tab on a piece of content you are editing, the Admin user may not have enabled versioning for the site or for the content type you are working with. Generally, though, versioning should be enabled. An Admin user can verify this by going to *Site Setup --> Types --> (your file type) -- Type Settings*. Verify that the *Versioned* check box is checked. Most of the time, this will already be checked. For more information, see the section called "Types" [212].

Solar System: Budget Vacation Resort

by Dick Solomon — last modified Jul 15, 2010 02:47 AM — History

If your content is being versioned, you will see a History hyperlink near the byline.
When you click **History**, you will see a pop-up dialog with the history of previous versions and its submission history, including any Change Notes that were made along with the revisions.

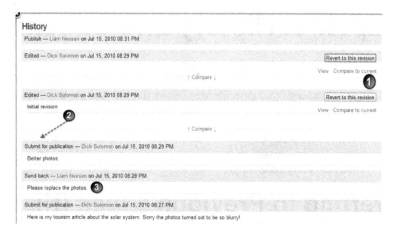

1.Compare to current lets you compare any version with the current one. Compare simply lets you compare two adjacent versions 2. History also stores workflow history. 3. Any Change Notes will be listed in history.

The **Revert to This Version** button lets you switch to a previously saved version of the same item. To be on the safe side, you probably should compare the older version with the newest one to make sure this is the version you want. The comparison screen uses color coding to show what is different:

- **Dark Green**. This shows any changes in HTML code (new paragraphs, etc.)

- **Pinkish Red**. This shows any content which was later deleted.

- **Light Green**. This shows text which was later added.

Inhabited Systems in the Introduction insert: `</h2>`

insert: `<p>`

It can sometimes be a bother to keep track of which star systems have life forms and which are warren wastelands. This reference guide will cover all life forms in the rowdy Milky Way galaxy (excluding psionic life forms). insert: `</p>`

insert: `<h2>`

Milky Way Galaxy

This reference guide will give an overview of a small number of bipedal. Please note that the Milky War has predominantly carbon-based life forms known to exist in the solar system. and most life forms prefer to stay within their own star systems (and yet tend to be mostly friendly to intergalactic travellers).

The Showing Differences Inline comparison feature uses color coding to let you see what has been added or changed.

Show Differences inline or as code? When you reach the Version/History page, you also have the option to Show Differences inline or as code. Inline is the default, and that is probably best for most cases (because it does highlight some HTML changes in dark green). Showing Differences as code will show you both versions in two separate columns and show only HTML code. It is not pretty, but the Code View makes it easier to spot what exactly has changed if the Inline view is unclear or insufficient.

Versioning and Deleted Items. Once you delete something, that item is gone for good. Even the history information is gone too.

Need to Undo a Mistake? You can revert to an older version if you have already saved, but what if you haven't saved yet? Don't forget that you also have the ability to use the browser's undo command (Control Z). See the section called "Playing it safe ...." [25].

Change Notes. On the bottom of every content item is a field for Change Notes. These notes are displayed when you press the History tab. While it is optional to make Change Notes, they can make it much easier to identify which version is the best to revert to.

As you might expect, Plone's history feature does increase the size of the database. The end of this chapter includes information about how to set reasonable limits about many versions to save.

One final thing. If your site has included and enabled the Save button on TinyMCE editor, using it to save items will <u>not</u> create a separate version of the item. A version is created only after you press the Save button at the bottom of the Edit area.

Page Locking

Plone uses a system of "soft locks" to prevent two users from overwriting one another's changes on the same content item. It is not foolproof, but it is functional and easy to understand.

When a content item is opened for editing, Plone will note this fact and warn anyone who tries to edit the same item that someone else has "locked this item for editing."

Plone's built in locking feature is not foolproof, but it does give an alert when another person is trying to edit the same document.

The second person to open the item has the choice to stop editing or to "break the lock" of the original person editing the item. As long as the second person waits until Dick Solomon finishes editing the document, things will go fine. But what if Dick Solomon starts editing, forgets about it and leaves the browser open the whole time? The second person will have no way of knowing whether Dick Solomon is still editing the content item or intends to do so. Conversely, the person who receives this lock message may decide to break the lock and start editing. In the worst case scenario, Dick Solomon could do a lot of editing, but when it comes time to save, he would overwrite Liam Neeson's changes after Liam overwrote Dick Solomon's changes. Sure, you could reconstruct the remnants of each edit by examining the entrails of previous versions, but that would be tedious.

Checking Out Working Copies of Published Items

Plone has a feature which allows one or more users to edit a temporary/private version of a content item which has already been published. It is called **Working Copy**.

Working Copy functionality is not installed by default, but it is included as an add on which must be enabled. To do that, the Plone Administrator must go to **Site Setup**, choose **Add Ons** and enable **Working Copy Support**.

After this is enabled, you will see the **Check Out** action appear in the drop-down menu for content items.

Figure 6.1. Checking Out Content

Checkout allows you to keep editing already published items

Although it is theoretically possible to check out private items, the most common situation where you use this feature is to check out a content item which has already been published.

When you check out an item, two things happen:

- Plone will protect the original (published) version from additional changes. The Edit option will no longer appear on the toolbar, even for users who have edit rights for the content.

- Plone will create a temporary working copy at a different temporary URL which is editable by one or more users. In other words, using a working copy does *not* give exclusive editing rights to a single individual. It merely protects the original URL of the item while the working copy is being edited. Even if the item were published before you checked out a working copy, the editable temporary copy will be in a **private** state.

You should see a Plone Locked message which describes who created the working copy, a link to the original URL and a link to the list of changes from the original version.

Figure 6.2. Checking out a Working Copy

Choosing the checkout option will create a temporary version of a published item for editing

After you check out a working copy, you will notice that the URL has changed. Note the differences:

- **http://www.pendelton.edu/academics/physics/dick-solomon-stuff/jello** *(the original item)*

- **http://www.pendelton.edu/academics/physics/dick-solomon-stuff/copy_of_jello** *(the working copy you are now editing)*

Working copies offer two advantages: They allow you to leave a published item untouched while you re-edit it. They also allow you to keep a change log of the private edits you are making to the working copy. This allows you to keep saving and editing until you have come up with a draft that you feel is polished enough to replace the current published version. **Remember:** the revision history will *not* go into the revision history for the original item.

When you have reached that point, you will simply check the item back in. (*Actions* --> *Check In*). Doing this will replace the "live" published version with the version you were editing as the working copy.

Working copies provide a good solution to the problem of having to edit something after being published. Because it allows you to work with a private version of a published item, there is a low risk of accidentally overwriting or ruining the published copy. Depending on your website's workflow, after you check something in, the content item will either be published directly or submitted for approval.

If you decide that you want to discard the working copy, simply choose *Actions* --> *Cancel Checkout*.

A Word to the Wise: Always Check Things In!

Warning: Even though you will be able to change the state of a working copy from Private to Published or Pending, don't do this until you first "check in" the working copy! (Actions --> Check In). If you publish a working copy without checking it in, you will be publishing a parallel (and nearly identical) version of the originally published item. That means you will now have two published versions, instead of replacing the original.

Advanced Topic: Limiting the version history

Earlier in this chapter, we covered how the history feature lets you compare the current revision of an item with previous versions and even to revert to an older version if necessary. Generally this feature works flawlessly.

Keeping all the versions of an item does, however, increase the size of Plone's database. While this should not affect your performance (and only indirectly if so), it may make sense to configure some reasonable defaults for how many versions which Plone saves for a content item. This will help to prevent the database from getting too large.

To set a purge policy for how many versions of a content item to save:

1. Log on as a user with the manager role.

2. Go to the ZMI by using the following path: **http://my-host.com/portal_purgepolicy** .

3. Enter a value in the field labeled **maximum number of versions to keep in storage (set to -1 for infinite)**.

4. Press the **Save Changes** button.

The default value is infinite (-1). Here are some things to keep in mind when setting a reasonable value here:

- Most users are probably only interested in the last 5-10 versions of an item.

- On items that you anticipate extensive editing, I would recommend setting 50 is a maximum limit for item versions.

- For most items, I would recommend setting the maximum versions to **20**. That is a good compromise between convenience and good database practices.

There are a few cases where leaving the value as infinite is recommended. If you are maintaining some kind of wiki, for example, then you may need to have a longer history. An infinite value would also be a desirable if your company is in an industry subject to audits, or where extensive recordkeeping is required.

Chapter 7. Sharing

Before you can have a collaborative editing environment, you must have a way to share editing rights with others. This chapter will cover how to give rights to users and how to use groups to enable sharing. The chapter concludes with an advanced topic about how to enable users who are not Admin users to manage the portlets in one or more folders.

Many of the tasks mentioned here require that you have Site Administrator or Manager rights. As mentioned in the book's introduction, this book will use the term **Admin user** for cases which apply to either the Site Administrator role or Manager role. There are slight differences between the two roles (and they will be described in the next section). For the most part, they can be used interchangeably.

Even if your user account does *not* have an Admin role, you might still see the Sharing tab for an individual content item. That allows you to view permissions for a particular item and grant (or remove) rights to it. These rights can be granted to a user or a group of users. This will be explained thoroughly in the section called "Assigning Rights for a Content Item to a User or Group (Sharing Tab)" [116].

Plone Roles

Each Plone role has a special set of permissions in the Plone workflow. Here are common Plone roles and what they mean:

- Contributor (can add content)

- Editor (can edit content by self or others. Can also delete a content item)

- Reader (can read content by others)

- Reviewer (can publish content and can edit items in a pending state)

- Manager (can access all the functions found on the Plone control panel and ZMI for the Plone instance; this is essentially the Administrator role)

- Site Administrator (can access the Plone control panel, but *cannot* install add-ons, edit themes or control system cache)

In 2011 Plone included an additional role out of the box: **Site Administrator**. From an organizational point of view, this new role makes it easier to delegate routine administrative functions to highly skilled users, without handing them the keys to the kingdom (so to speak). For example, the Site Administrator has the ability to edit both users and groups. The Site Administrator can resolve routine sharing/permission problems, add/edit portlets, customize folder views, edit collections and edit content rules. All of these actions are performed entirely within the Plone interface and don't necessarily require programming or system administration skills. In this book, when we use the term "Admin user," we generally mean *both* the Manager and Site Administrator role.

On the control panel's *Users and Groups* menu, these terms are not used interchangeably, so that might cause some confusion. For example, on the *User's Overview* menu, there is a column for **Site Administrator** and **Manager**, but on the *Add New User* pop-up menu, you will notice that two default groups have already been created: **Administrators** and **Site Administrators**. Don't panic! When you add a new user to the **Administrator** group, that user will have the role of **Manager**.

Note the differences between a Reviewer and an Editor. An Editor simply has the right to edit the same item as the original content creator plus the right to delete it. But a Reviewer has the right to change the state of a content item (usually from Pending to Publish). During the time when a content item is in this pending state, a user with the Reviewer role also gains the temporary ability to edit the item and its properties.

As we've covered above, when a content item has been submitted, the Reviewer gains the temporary ability to edit the content item. This ability ends after the state of the item has changed (to Private or Published). Even though a user with the Reviewer role gains the temporary ability to edit a content item, that does not include the ability to delete that content item.

A user can have this role globally or only for a certain folder or content item. Later this chapter will cover how to use the Share tab to give another user a right to serve as Contributor/Editor/Reviewer for a single folder or content item.

Assigning Global Roles to Users

The process of assigning a role to users is straightforward, but remember that only Admin users have this right.

1. Go to **Site Setup** (you must have the Manager role to be able to do this). **Choose Users and Groups**.

2. Find the user name on the user list. If it is not visible, you will need to enter the name in the search box and press **Search**.

3. On the role, add a check to the box of the Global role you wish this to add and click **Apply Changes**.

This approach is useful in assigning roles for smaller sites, with fewer than 10 or 20 users, but the problem is that these roles apply everywhere on the site. If you gave a user the Contributor role, for example, he or she would be able to add content *anywhere* on the site, which could be problematic. If a user is given Edit rights for a folder, that also means that this user has the ability to **delete** any content item inside this same folder! Because of the potentially destructive powers that comes with the Editor role, it should be rare for a user to be given Editor as a global role. Instead, a user is included in a group which is granted the Editor role for certain folders only.

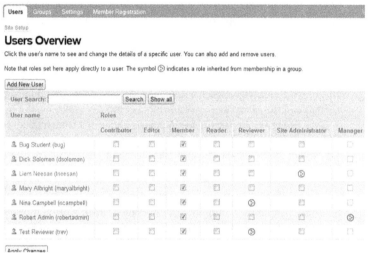

The user Liam Neeson is manager because he belongs to the Administrators group. Nina Campbell is a global Reviewer because she belongs to the Reviewers group.

This is why, instead of assigning global roles to users, Admin users will generally create groups with pre-assigned roles.

Creating a Group

When the Admin user adds or edits a user account, one necessary step is assigning this user to an existing group.

The Admin can create a new group fairly easily. Go to **Site Setup --> Users & Groups.** On the navigation bar in the middle of the page, choose **Groups.** On this URL (called *Groups Overview*), there will be a button, **Add New Group**, which does exactly that. Here are some guidelines for adding a new group.

- The **Name** field does not allow spaces (it will give an error if you do). This field is basically assigning a unique value for the database, and it will usually not be seen. The second **Title** field, however, can contain multiple words and should be as descriptive as possible. This field is what Admins see when configuring users and groups.

- An out-of-the-box Plone instance usually comes with several global roles already: Administrators, Reviewers and Site Administrators. There is no need to create new groups that duplicate these groups.

- Although the *Groups Overview* lets you add global roles to group members of your new group, it is perfectly acceptable for the Admin user to not check any of the global role boxes for a particular group. Why? Many Admin users may find it best not to give global roles to users or groups; instead these rights can be added to a group or user via the Sharing tab for the appropriate Plone folder.

Adding a User to a Group (Admin Only)

Plone lets you put a user into one or more groups. You can do this from the same Users and Groups screen on *Site Setup*. Consider the case of Nina Campbell, the department administrator for the Physics department. Suppose we wanted to add her to a group with the global ability to approve content (i.e., the global Reviewer role) and the ability to access a special HR folder.

1. When logged in as an Admin user, go to **Site Setup** and go to the **Users and Groups** tab.

2. Find the name Nina Campbell in the user list. If it is not shown, you may need to use the search box to find it.

3. After the name Nina Campbell appears, click on her name (it will be a hyperlink).

4. Switch to the **Group Memberships** tab.

At this point, you will see her list of current group memberships and a list of possible groups which she could also join.

Personal Information   Personal Preferences   **Group Memberships**

Group memberships for Nina Campbell (ncampbell)

Up to Users Overview

Current group memberships

Group Name	Remove
🏢 Authenticated Users (Virtual Group)	☐
🏢 Physics Staff	☐

[Remove from selected groups]

Assign to groups

	Group/User name
☐	🏢 Administrators
☐	🏢 Faculty Members
☐	🏢 Generic permissions for students
☑	🏢 HR Staff & Administration
☐	🏢 Portlet Managers
☑	🏢 Reviewers

[Add user to selected groups]

Users can belong to more than one group.

Assigning Global Roles to Groups

Generally you should <u>not</u> assign a global role to either a user or a group. Instead, the user or group should be granted rights on the *Sharing* tab of the relevant folder(s) in question. For performance reasons, it is not recommended to assign a right to a specific user or group at the Plone root folder. Any changes to rights at root will require a full re-indexing of every object on the site. If you must share at the root folder, you should share with a group and not specific users. Then, if you need to modify who is assigned these rights, you simply can add or remove members to this group in *Site Setup --> Users and Groups* without re-indexing.

Plone permissions are normally handled through Plone groups. On *Site Setup* you can assign a global role to a group (and all its constituent members). Look at the group configuration page:

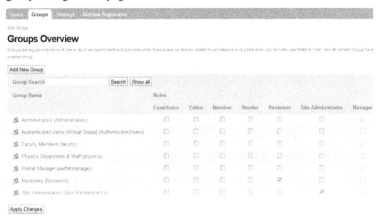

It is common for groups not to have any global roles assigned to it.

At first it might seem strange for a group to have no global roles. What would be the point of having it? A group with no global roles can still have permissions assigned to it at the folder or item level. This will be covered in the next section.

An often-overlooked benefit of configuring groups is the ability to create group portlets which appear only to members of a specified group. Suppose a university site assigned all students to a group. On the Users & Groups control panel, the Admin user could select the specific Students group, click the **Group Portlets** tab and configure a portlet which would be visible only to members of the Students group. This could be used to show content relevant to all students. For more information, see the section called the section called "Group Portlets" [165].

Assigning Rights for a Content Item to a User or Group (Sharing Tab)

On content items and folders the primary toolbar will have an option for sharing. The Sharing tab lets you manually assign the right to add/edit/review content to groups or user(s) at this specific Plone folder.

Suppose that you are a university with a folder for the physics department. Obviously you don't want everyone to add or edit content, and conversely you don't want adding or editing to be limited only to those with global roles of Contributor, Editor, or Reviewer. Instead, you can use the Sharing tab to add a specific group or user to a folder. This is why some groups won't need to have global roles; you are assigning roles to groups by using the Sharing tab.

The process for assigning rights via the Sharing tab is easy. First, create a group named "Physics Staff." Then, go to the folder named "Physics". When logged in as the folder owner or Admin user, click the *Sharing* tab. From there, you can add the Physics Staff group (by typing the group name in the Search box) and assign this group the *Can Add* right to this folder by checking the box in the appropriate column.

A few remarks:

- The Sharing tab does not list everyone with rights to the selected folder. It only lists names of users and groups which have been manually added to this specific folder. For example, Nina Campbell has the global role as Reviewer, but her name is not listed here. Users granted rights within a certain folder as a result of membership in a group with a global role (e.g., Administrators, Authenticated Users) will not be listed on a folder's Sharing tab.

- Sometimes Plone will give an error message when you try to grant a permission. This happens because you do not have the right to grant this permission.

- The Sharing tab shows the names of both Groups and Users.

- If **Inherit permissions from higher levels** is unchecked, and if the user inherited rights to a folder from membership in a group with a global role, they must be removed from this group (or the group must be modified) in order to restrict access to the folder.

- Removing a check from a user's role on an item's Sharing tab does not automatically remove the permission itself. If the user had this permission through a global role or if the user received this permission as result of membership in a group, this user may still possess this right.

Who can view the Sharing tab?

Any user who adds a content item will automatically receive the right to edit it (unless the item has been submitted for publication, in which case the item will not be editable until it has been approved for publication). When a user has editing rights for a content item, he or she will see **Edit** listed as an option on the toolbar above the content item itself. When you have Edit rights, you will also see other options listed as well (such as **Sharing** and **Syndication**).

You might assume that only a user with Admin rights would have the right to use the Sharing tab of a folder or content item. Actually, anyone who already has a certain role within a folder would also have the right to view the Sharing tab and share this right to another user or group. Suppose ordinary user Dick Solomon is a physics professor who added a folder called "Dick Solomon Stuff." If he wanted to give a student named "Bug" the right to edit a single document inside the "Dick Solomon Stuff" folder, Dick could simply go to the Sharing tab for the item, search for Bug's user account and manually give him edit permissions, as shown below.

Figure 7.1. Using the Sharing Tab to let another user edit a page

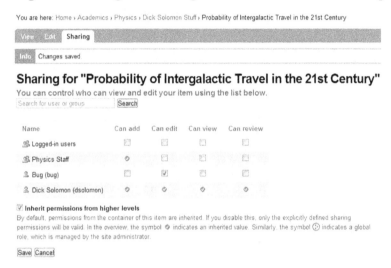

Because Dick Solomon has full rights to the Dick Solomon stuff folder, he can give a student the edit permissions to one of his pages.

Even if Dick Solomon hadn't created the actual document but had simply been granted edit rights to it by another faculty member, he could still assign the same edit rights to Bug. But Plone prevents you from adding or removing a user's right if your user account didn't have the right in the first place.

Full Rights & Folder Ownership

When a user creates a folder, that user has the Add/Edit/View rights to contents in this folder. But the Review right is *not* automatically granted to the folder owner. It must be granted by the Admin user manually because the "Review" right is the right to change an item's state to Published. If an owner were automatically granted the right to promote one of his items to Published, that would essentially circumvent the whole workflow process.

The owner/creator of a folder has the ability to view the Sharing tab and share Add/Edit/View rights to any user. If the owner or creator of a folder has Review rights, he or she can also share this Review right with another user.

Finally, the owner/creator of a folder has the right to turn off permissions granted to other people in this folder. If the Admin user checks the boxes for Add/Edit rights to a folder for another user, the owner/creator still has the ability to uncheck those same rights on the Sharing tab. More importantly, the owner/creator of a folder has the right to uncheck the *Inherit Permissions from higher levels* option. Unchecking this option will remove any rights which were granted in a parent folder.

Who is the owner of the folder? Assuming that no one has edited the Creator's field, the byline will show which user created the content object.

Inheriting permissions from higher levels

This part can be confusing, so don't worry if it takes some time for the concept to sink in. Below is a simple example of how inherited permissions work:

Suppose you have a **Physics** folder, and a group called "Physics Staff" was given the rights to add content to this folder.

Inside the Physics folder is another folder called **Dick Solomon Stuff**. *Question:* Would users in the Physics Staff group have the ability to add content in the **Dick Solomon Stuff** folder?

Answer: Yes, because permissions from Dick Solomon Stuff folder are inherited from the Physics folder. Here is what the Sharing tab for Dick Solomon Stuff will look like:

Figure 7.2. Inheriting Permissions from a Higher Folder

You are here: Home › Academics › Physics › Dick Solomon Stuff

| Contents | View | Edit | **Sharing** |

Sharing for "Dick Solomon Stuff"

You can control who can view and edit your item using the list below.

| Search for user or group | [Search] |

Name	Can add	Can edit	Can view	Can review
🙎 Logged-in users	☐	☐	☐	☐
🙎 Physics Staff	⊘	☐	☐	☐
🙎 Bug (bug)	☑	☐	☐	☐
🙎 Dick Solomon (dsolomon)	☑	⊘	☑	☑

☑ **Inherit permissions from higher levels**
By default, permissions from the container of this item are inherited. If you disable this, only the explicitly defined sharing permissions will be valid. In the overview, the symbol ⊘ indicates an inherited value. Similarly, the symbol ⊕ indicates a global role, which is managed by the site administrator.

[Save] [Cancel]

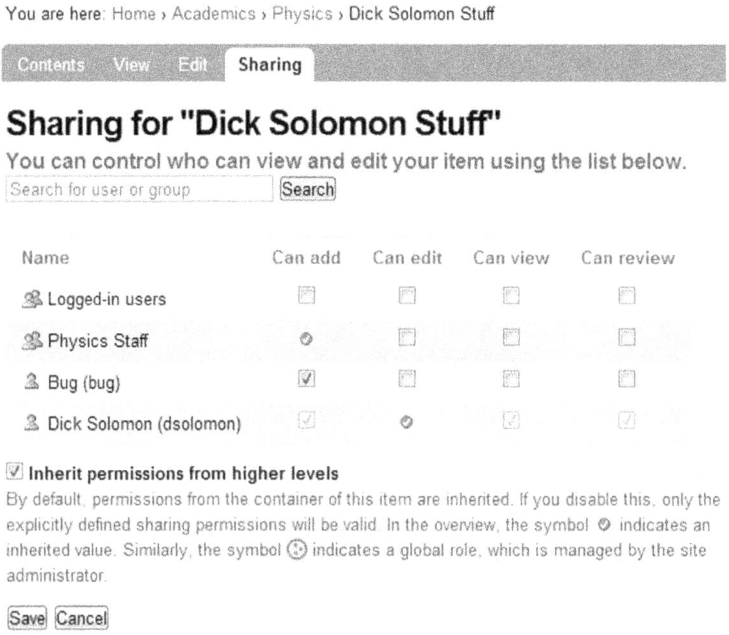

Physics Staff has the inherited right to add content in the Dick Solomon Stuff folder.

As you can see, the green circle with a checkmark is placed beside the *Can Add* permission for "Physics Staff", which indicates the permission has been inherited from a folder at a higher level. Dick Solomon is a member of the Physics Staff group, so he is already allowed to add a folder or page into the Physics folder, and would definitely have the right to add content the "Dick Solomon Stuff" folder there. But who else would have that right?

Let's say another user, Nina Campbell, is also a member of the "Physics Staff" group. Would she have the ability to add content into the "Dick Solomon Stuff" folder? Yes, because she inherited the *Can Add* permissions from her Physics Staff membership. Would she have the ability to edit a page created by Dick Solomon? No, because her group membership only allows her to add content. In fact, Nina Campbell will not even see the Sharing tab when inside the Dick Solomon Stuff folder.

In Figure 7.2, " Inheriting Permissions from a Higher Folder" [120], we notice that Dick Solomon is listed on the Sharing tab. But if Dick Solomon is already a member of the "Physics Staff" group, why would his name be listed separately? We see that *Can Review* is listed as a permission for Dick Solomon but *Can Add* / *Can Edit* / *Can View* are all unchecked.

In fact, if you are the owner/creator of a folder, you will not normally see permissions for *Can Add /Can Edit / Can View*. They are implied. The *Can Review* box was checked because the Admin user had manually checked the *Can Review* box for Dick Solomon in this folder.

The point of this rather convoluted example is simply to illustrate that it is sometimes hard to figure out why the permissions on a content item look the way they do. Although Plone has a tight security model, it is not always obvious how to correct a permission problem.

Warning: The *Can Edit* permission for a folder is dangerous!

If you give a user the *Can Edit* right to a folder via the Sharing tab, you are also giving that person the right to delete *every single item inside the folder*. Because you can't undo something you have deleted, the *Can Edit* permission for a folder should not be shared unless you have absolute trust in the user receiving this right and have accepted the possibility that this user could potentially damage the entire contents of that folder. Award this right carefully!

Technically speaking, a user with the Manager role could undo one or more deletes (especially if it is caught relatively soon thereafter). See the section called the section called "Undoing Deleted Content " [124] for how to do this. But depending on the specific sequence of actions, it may not always be possible to undo delete operations.

Removing Inherited Permissions

A check mark inside a green circle indicates you are viewing a permission which has been granted in a higher folder. In the illustration above, "Physics Staff" has the inherited right to add content to this folder. When folder owner Dick Solomon unchecks the **Inherit Permissions from Higher Levels** option, he can remove those same rights. Let's see the result:

Figure 7.3. Disabling the inheritance of permissions

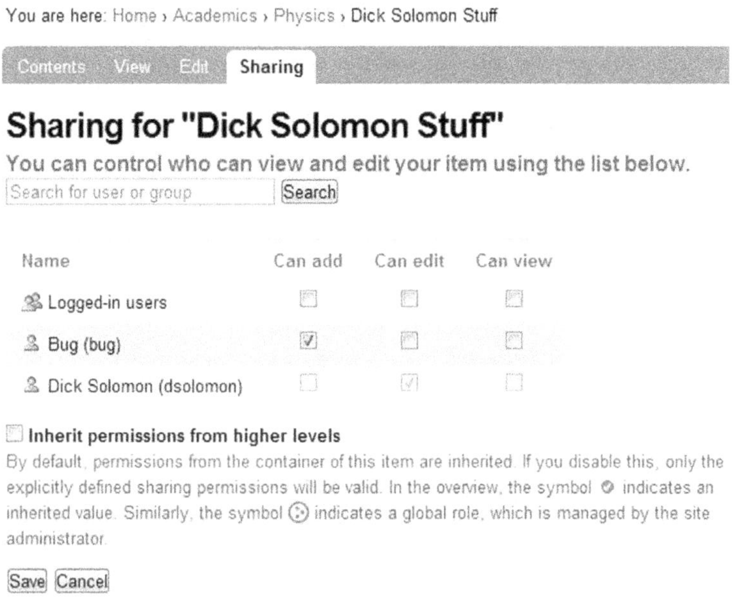

You are here: Home › Academics › Physics › Dick Solomon Stuff

| Contents | View | Edit | **Sharing** |

Sharing for "Dick Solomon Stuff"

You can control who can view and edit your item using the list below.

| Search for user or group | [Search] |

Name	Can add	Can edit	Can view
👥 Logged-in users	☐	☐	☐
👤 Bug (bug)	☑	☐	☐
👤 Dick Solomon (dsolomon)	☐	☑	☐

☐ **Inherit permissions from higher levels**

By default, permissions from the container of this item are inherited. If you disable this, only the explicitly defined sharing permissions will be valid. In the overview, the symbol ⊘ indicates an inherited value. Similarly, the symbol ⊙ indicates a global role, which is managed by the site administrator.

[Save] [Cancel]

When you uncheck the "inherit permissions" option, the only permissions will be what the owner specifies for this folder.

The permissions for the Physics Staff have now disappeared. New members of the Physics Staff group can no longer add content to Dick Solomon's folder.

(The only exception is global roles – roles which are controlled only by the Admin user and cannot be overridden on the Sharing tab).

What are the permissions of the "Dick Solomon Stuff" folder now that the inherited permissions have been disabled?

- Dick Solomon has complete rights to add/edit/delete content and even to assign permissions to other users and groups.

- Bug has the ability to add content in the Dick Solomon folder.

- No one in the group Physics Staff has the ability to add or edit content in this folder.

Removing a right from a user

It is not common for global roles/rights to be assigned via *Site Setup --> Users and Groups*. Instead, the Admin user typically assigns users to groups on this menu without assigning roles. If these global roles are assigned, they cannot be removed for individual folders. As long as a user belongs to a global role either on the Users or the Groups tab in *Site Setup*, he will have all the rights belonging to that global role.

As said before, it is best not to assign global roles to users or groups; you usually assign various rights to a user or group on a specific folder or content item. If you wish to remove a right from a user, you cannot be completely sure that the right has been removed unless you have verified that that the right isn't a global role assigned on the *Users & Groups* configuration screen.

How then could we be sure that user Dick Solomon no longer has (for example) the edit right to a certain folder?

1. On the *Users & Groups* configuration screen of *Site Setup* (visible to Admin users only), verify that Dick Solomon has not received the global role of Editor.

2. On the Sharing tab for that folder, verify that Dick Solomon does not have the edit right granted to him for the specific folder AND

3. On that same tab, verify that none of the groups which Dick Solomon belongs to has the edit right for the specific folder AND

4. On that same tab, verify that neither Dick Solomon nor any group Dick Solomon belongs to has inherited the right to edit this folder.

In the Sharing tab for that folder, if you see a green circle with a checkmark by a permission, that means that a user or group has **inherited** a right from a higher folder. If you see a blue circle with 3 dots, that means that the permission is granted as a result of a global role (and so it can only be changed by an Admin user on *Site Setup*).

Advanced Topics

There are two content-related actions which Admin users might have to perform: deleting content and undoing deletes.

Deleting Content

Deleting content is not difficult to do, but some details should be explained to prevent avoidable accidents. There are two ways to delete content:

1. You can delete an item by clicking *Actions --> Delete* when you are editing it. **Note:**If you do not see Delete as an option here, it means you do not have the rights to delete.

2. You can delete one or more content items inside a folder by clicking the **Contents** tab, selecting one or more items and clicking the **Delete** button.

If you are the content owner or creator, you can generally delete your own content. Keep in mind that some sites' workflows may be customized to prevent deletions, even from the content owner/creator.

If you delete a content item, you do *not* have the ability to access an earlier version of the same content.

When you delete a content item by clicking *Actions --> Delete*, you will be prompted with a confirmation dialogue. However, when you delete one or more items from the Contents tab of a folder, you will receive no warning or confirmation dialogue.

If a user has the right to edit a folder, that also means that the user has the right to delete all the contents for a folder. For this reason, this right shouldn't be granted liberally.

Sometimes when you are deleting a content item, you may receive a message that *"Deleting this item will break links that exist in the items listed below"*. This is the link integrity feature built into Plone. See the section called "Advantages of using internal links " [43].

Undoing Deleted Content

Many users have grown used to having a Trashcan or Recycle Bin from which deleted content can be easily restored. Unfortunately, in content management systems like Plone, undoing deleted content isn't as easy. Sometimes, in fact, there is no pop-up to ask you to confirm a deletion.

Plone allows users to undo individual edits and revert to a previous edit. (*For more, see the section called "Reverting to Previous Saves (History)" [104]*). In addition, an *Undo* button on the rich text editor (or pressing Ctl-Z) can undo individual edits before saving. But once an item is deleted, there is no longer any history associated with it.

Plone's security model is strict enough to prevent a user from deleting content by others. But if you are logged in as an Admin user, you can potentially do a lot of damage with an accidental deletion.

Fortunately a user with the manager role has the ability to undo individual deletes. As long as the user undoes the delete action relatively soon after the mistake has been made, the undoing process is fairly simple. It requires going into the Zope Management Interface (ZMI).

To undo a delete action:

1. As a user with the Manager role, go into the ZMI. Typically you can do this by adding "/manage" to the end of the root URL. (For example, *www.pendelton.edu/manage*).

2. Verify that you are at the root for the Plone site in the ZMI. Typically, the top of the right panel will say, **"Plone Site at /"**.

3. On the right panel of the ZMI, there will be several tabs along the top. (*Contents, Components, View, etc.*) Click on the **Undo** tab. If you do not see the Undo tab, it's probably because you are not at Plone root (and will need to go up or down a level to do so).

4. The right panel will show the last 20 changes made to the Plone site, the URL where the change was made and a date stamp. Look for a change listing which starts with the word "Deleted."

5. After you have found the change listing containing the deletion you wish to undo, check the box beside it and click the **Undo** button at the bottom. You can check several boxes, although typically you will only need to check one box.

What happens if you cannot find the deletion in the 20 transactions shown here? The date stamp column on right has a clickable link for **Earlier Transactions**. By clicking this link, you can look through even earlier transactions to find the one you want. Unfortunately, the ZMI does not provide a way to show only deleted items on the transaction list, so you will need to manually go back 20 transactions at a time. For this reason, the sooner you try to undo a deletion, the easier it will be to find it. Sometimes a later action might be incompatible with executing an Undo command, so the ZMI may not be able to undo it, if later transactions have modified objects that were modified by a selected transaction.

Fortunately though, if you delete a folder containing a lot of subfolders with additional items and subfolders, you need only to undo one Delete action to restore the folder and its contents.

Giving Group Members the rights to manage or add Portlets in certain folders

The ability to manage portlets is helpful for power users to have. When Plone is first set up, ordinary content creators will not normally have the ability to manage what portlets display on a content item, or what folder they are working on. It's relatively easy, however, for a user with the Manager role to give users the right to modify the portlets which appear on the left or right of their content. For more about portlets, see Chapter 10, *Managing Portlets* [152].

In general, Plone is a very locked down CMS, and the same is true with your ability to add and edit portlets. By default, ordinary users (including Content Creators, Editors and Reviewers) do not have the rights to edit or configure portlets. Only an Admin user has the ability to manage portlets globally. Managers can also delegate to certain users the right to manage portlets on folder contents for which he or she has access. To do this, Managers will need to go into the Zope Management Interface (ZMI) and make a simple customization.

You need to be logged on as a user with the Manager role before performing delegations:

1. The user with the Manager role should go to the folder URL. For this example, it will be *www.pendelton.edu/academics/physics/* . Add "manage_access" (with the underscore between the two words) to the end of the folder URL. In this case, the URL would then be *www.pendelton.edu/academics/physics/manage_access*. To reach this address, you will manually need to type the phrase *manage_access* after the folder URL. Alternatively, this page can be reached by going to Site Setup --> Zope Management Interface, and then clicking on the "Security" tab along the top of the screen.

2. You will see a long list of permissions. Most, if not all, of these permissions will be blank. On the **Reviewer** column, make sure these options are checked: **Portlets: Manage Portlets, plone.portlet.collection: Add collection portlet, plone.portlet.static: Add static portlet**. Do Not Touch anything else! Press **Save**.

3. While still logged on as the Manager, go to **Plone Site Setup** and choose **Users and Groups**.

4. Click the **Groups** tab. Click the **Add New Group** button. In your new group, make the **name** Physics Portlet Managers and **title** Physics Portlet Managers. Press **Save**. **Note:** for this example, you will *not* give the Physics Portlet Manager groups any roles.

5. Now it is to time to assign a user to be a member of this group. In this example, we will create a new user, but you can just as easily add an existing user to the Portlet Manager group. Click on the User tab and click the button Add New User. The full name will be Mary Albright and the username will be malbright. At the bottom of the dialog will be an option **Add to the following groups**. Choose the **Physics Portlet Manager** group and nothing else.

6. Now the user with the Manager role will navigate to the folder which members of the Physics Portlet Manager group need the right to manage/add portlets to. In this case, it is in the /academics/physics directory for the site.

7. Choose the **Sharing** tab. While logged on as the Admin user, type the name "Physics Portlet Manager" into the Search field and press the Search button. The group name will appear below on the list.

8. For the row corresponding to Physics Portlet Manager, select **Can Review**. (It is *not* required to select *Can View*. However, *Can View* will allow a user who belongs to the Physics Portlet Manager group to view public as well as draft documents).

9. Press **Save**.

At this point, Mary Albright (or any member in the Physics Portlet Manager group) will be able to manage any portlets for the physics folder (and subfolders). Whenever any member of the Portlet Managers group goes to this folder, they will see a small wide gray rectangle at the bottom left and bottom right of the screen which says **Manage Portlets**.

For this example, we assume that you need to create a new group to have the Reviewer role for the physics folder. However, as an alternate method, instead of creating a new group, you could simply use an existing group, such as "Physics Staff". If you were doing that, when you went to the Sharing tab, you would search for Physics Staff group and give to that group the **Can Review** right by checking the appropriate box. The main advantage of having a separate group for this is that a Physics staff member wouldn't necessarily need to have the Reviewer permission as well.

Giving individual members the rights to manage or add Portlets in certain folders

The process of giving individuals rights to manage a portlet in a certain folder is similar to the process of giving rights to a group. After you make sure that the Reviewer role has the portlet-related permissions enabled inside the folder, you will add a user to the Sharing tab of the folder and give it *Can Review* permissions. You need to be logged on as a user (with the Manager role) to go to the *manage_access* view.

1. The user with the Manager role should go to the folder URL. For this example, it will be *www.pendelton.edu/academics/physics/* . Add "manage_access" to the end of the folder URL. In this case, the URL would then be *www.pendelton.edu/academics/physics/manage_access*. To reach this address, you will need to type manage_access manually at the end of the folder URL.

2. You will see a long list of permissions. Most, if not all, of the permissions will be blank. On the **Reviewer** column, make sure all five options are checked. **Portlets: Manage Own Portlets**, **Portlets: Manage Portlets**, **Portlets: View Dashboard**, **plone.portlet.collection: Add collection portlet**, **plone.portlet.static: Add static portlet**. Do Not Touch anything else! Press **Save**.

3. Now the Admin user can navigate to the Physics department folder. *www.pendelton.edu/academics/physics/*

4. Choose the **Sharing** tab. While logged on as the Admin user, type the name "Vincent Strudwick" or "Strudwick" into the Search field and press the Search button. The user's name will appear below on the list.

5. For the row corresponding to Vincent Strudwick, select **Can Review**. (It is *not* required to select *Can View*. However, *Can View* will allow Vincent Strudwick to view published documents as well as draft documents).

6. Press **Save**.

At this point, Vincent Strudwick will be able to manage any portlets for the Physics Department folder, and its subfolders. Whenever Vincent Strudwick visits this folder or its subfolders, he will see a small wide rectangle at the bottom left and bottom right of the screen which says **Manage Portlets**.

This method allows one user to have the ability to manage portlets for a single folder (and its subfolders). If you expect to give this same right to several users, you might wish to create a separate group for it instead.

Chapter 8. Collaborative Editing: Workflows

Now that we have established that multiple users can share and edit documents, it is time to discuss the publication sequence, which we will refer to as "workflow".

A content management system like Plone provides a good working space for users to collaborate in the publishing process. But a new web application can present complexities, growing pains, and can disrupt how people do things – for better or worse. If you were previously working with another content management system, you could encounter a variety of other issues, such as formatting problems with legacy content, or finding that the new way of doing things involves more steps, and/or an alternate approach.

Plone offers a very centralized solution, geared toward oversight and interdependence in collaboration. Content creators who are used to a decentralized publishing process are, frankly, used to a process that is unnecessarily slow. While Plone may have a learning curve, once learned, content creators will enjoy greater efficiency and quality of collaboration versus decentralized approaches.

Content creators don't normally need to worry about setting up workflow; that is the Admin user's or the site developer's job. But this chapter might help the content creator understand why Plone works the way that it does. It also might explain why the publishing process may not go as smoothly as expected, and offer options for tackling these problems.

In May 2010 Plone developer and trainer Joel Burton gave a fantastic 30 minute talk at a Plone conference about Plone workflows. This talk was videotaped and is listed in the book's recommended links at **http://www.enfoldsystems.com/support/a-users-guide-to-plone.html**. It is a terrific introduction to the subject.

Key Concepts

Plone offers a variety of publication sequences, depending on how the site planners set up your site. Admin users can even customize workflows so they are tailored to your site's needs. But because the focus of this book is content creation and not administration, we will not cover this subject in great depth. The end of this chapter will include a brief discussion about advanced tweaks you can make to the publication sequence. Also, Appendix A, *Basic Plone Workflows* [223] contains a brief listing of all the available default workflows.

Aside from images or file uploads, **when a person adds a content item somewhere and starts editing it, it will be in a private state**. No matter how many times he or she presses Save, the item will remain in the private state until the user decides to publish it, or submit it for approval.

No matter how many times you save an item, it will remain in a private state until you change the state to Submit/Advanced/Publish.

Depending on how the site was set up, you might publish a content item immediately or submit it for approval. If that is the case, someone with the Reviewer role will need to change the state for you. Refer to the previous chapter on the section called "Plone Roles " [111].

The website uses colored fonts to indicate state. Of course, your organization's site might use customized colors, but here are the default colors you'll typically encounter:

- **red** – private state

- **orange** – pending

- **navy blue** – published

Even after a content item has been published, the content creator or Reviewer can send it back into a private state again.

One notable exception to this color coding occurs when a collection portlet displays private or pending items. The collection itself will still show the same color coding; only the collection portlet displays collection results without color coding.

Workflows may vary from site to site, but **generally the workflow depends on the content type**. All pages follow the same workflow sequence, and events will follow the workflow. This does not mean, however, that workflows for different content types must necessarily be different. Often, many of the content types for a site are configured to use identical workflows. Some add-ons (like Placeful Workflows) can impact workflow as well.

Visibility of Items

Site visitors will see published items, but keep in mind Plone hides private and draft items from site visitors and generally even from logged-in users.

It can be confusing to understand why some items are visible to logged-in users and why others are not. This can be a concern when Plone's search might permit users to locate content items which were placed in obscure, or non intuitive folders on the site.

The workflow designates who is able to view an item on a website and under what conditions. It distinguishes between items which can only be viewed by their authors and those which can be freely viewed by logged in users or visitors.

- Admin users can generally see all content items, and even private items.

- **Published items in private folders are still published.** Keeping published items inside a private folder is generally not a good idea for usability reasons. Although the folder itself will remain private, users will be able to see that the Published item belongs to its containing folder, which is otherwise hidden.

- **Items in a folder are not guaranteed to be private even if the folder is marked private.** Some kinds of content, like images or files, are typically not given a workflow state and depend on the state of its container. So if a folder contains images and the folder is private, the images inside this folder will also usually be private. On the other hand, a page inside a private folder can certainly be published.

- **Visibility (and workflow in general) is configurable.** Although images don't have workflow states by default, in some cases, an organization may wish to require all images to have a workflow so they can be approved by a Reviewer.

Hiding Items from Portlets and Search Results

The state of an item determines who is allowed to view it. Each item put through the workflow process possesses a state, and this state can be changed along the course of the workflow process by authors and Editors.

The Admin user has the ability to hide items (in certain workflow states) from portlets, the site's search, and the site map.

To hide items from navigation portlets and the site map, go to *Site Setup -->* *Navigation* and enable the option **Filter on workflow state**. From there, you can specify workflow states of items which are allowed to appear in portlets, including:

- Externally visible [external]

- Internal draft [internal]

- Internally published [internally_published]

- Pending review [pending]

- Private [private]

- Public draft [visible]

- Published [published]

If you enable this option, you can hide content items which are pending review, while leaving internally published and published items visible.

To hide specific content types from search results, go to *Site Setup* --> *Search* and unselect the boxes for the content types you don't wish to appear in search results.

Getting it Published: The Stages

The stages of getting something published can vary. Your organization may use a customized workflow or the labels for the states may differ from the default ones.

Items generally start out as **private**. What this means might vary according to your workflow, but generally it means that no one can see else your content item except Admin users, users with edit rights to your document and anyone else you may have shared the document with.

Your website may be configured so that you are not able to publish items as you please. In that case, you would need to change the state of the item to **Submit**. After you do this, the state will change from **Private** to **Pending**. For certain publication workflows, the content creator can choose **Publish** directly from the state drop-down list. In some cases, Submit may not be listed as an option, and this simply means that for this particular item in this particular location, the inter-mediary step of Submit/Pending has been removed.

The only way for a pending item to be published is for someone with Reviewer rights to change its state from **Pending** to **Published**. *Note:* the Reviewer role is not the same thing as an Editor. For more, see the section called "Plone Roles " [111]. An Editor simply shares the right to edit content with the original content creator, but the Editor does not necessarily have the ability to change the item's state. A Reviewer, on the other hand, does have this right and is the final arbiter of scheduling when the content item is actually published.

If the item has been already been published and the content creator decides it need to be "unpublished," he can choose the **Retract** action. Doing so will change the state of the item from **Published** to **Private** again. If the Reviewer wishes to "unpublish" an item, he will choose the **Send Back** action from the State list. This was called "Reject" in 3.0 workflows, and in some deployments, this label was changed to the less judgmental "Hide."

Generally, a content item can be published and retracted numerous times. The workflow in Plone is made up of a certain number of states which an item can retain and a sequence of transitions between these states. These are referred to as "workflow states" and "state changes."

Some items do not have states (and do not need to be submitted or published)

As stated earlier, some content types do not normally have states, but they will always appear as published unless they are in a private folder. By default, the image content type and file type (.PDF, .DOC, etc) have no workflow states, so you do not need to worry about submitting them or publishing them.

Workflow History

Plone creates a log recording all of the state changes made to each item, along with any comments added by users. As soon as a change is made to the workflow state, or when any comments about the workflow are added, it will appear on the changelog (as well as on a list of the edited versions which have been stored). For more information, see the section called "Reverting to Previous Saves (History)" [104].

Submitting Content

One of the drop-down options under State is **Submit**. When you choose this option, the state will change to Pending, and the font color will turn to Orange (assuming the site uses the default colors). You can generally still edit your content while it is pending, but make certain that the Reviewer is not also simultaneously editing the same content item.

Another option under State is **Advanced**. This all-purpose option allows you to change the state, schedule publications, and attach a note from one dialog. For this reason, it's a good idea to select the Advanced option regardless of the change you wish to make to the state.

Figure 8.1. Advanced State Dialog

Publishing process

An item's status (also called its review state) determines who can see it. Another way to control the visibility of an item is with its *Publishing Date*. An item is not publicly searchable before its publishing date. This will prevent the item from showing up in portlets and folder listings, although the item will still be available if accessed directly via its URL.
Affected content

	Title	Size	Modified	State
☑	📄 Solar System: Budget Vacation Resort	1 kB	Jul 15, 2010 02:47 AM	Private

Publishing Date
The date when the item will be published. If no date is selected the item will be published immediately.

2010 ▾ / August ▾ / 1 ▾ ▦ -- ▾ : -- ▾ -- ▾

Expiration Date
The date when the item expires. This will automatically make the item invisible for others at the given date. If no date is chosen, it will never expire

-- ▾ / -- ▾ / -- ▾ ▦ -- ▾ : -- ▾ -- ▾

Comments
Will be added to the publishing history. If multiple items are selected, this comment will be attached to all of them

Here is my tourism article about the solar system. Sorry that the photographs turned out to be so blurry!

Change State
Select the transition to be used for modifying the items state
○ No change
◉ Submit for publication

[Save] [Cancel]

Advanced state tab lets you add notes and propose or authorize a publishing date

Reviewing, Approving & Scheduling Content

Reviewers are on the receiving end of submitted content, and they are responsible for sending back or approving content. Sometimes the reviewing process is pro forma, which ensures that a responsible person has seen the content at least once. Sometimes the reviewing process will involve a step where the Reviewer vigorously examines the content item and makes changes where necessary. The depth of the review may depend on the content and the needs of the organization, as well as the people involved. Keep in mind that the Reviewer can be a bottleneck for publication, if too many things need to be submitted. In his May 2010 talk at Plone Symposium East, Joel Burton noted 2 things about the Plone reviewing process:

- Submit for review should not be a required step unless circumstances require it. When too much content is being submitted, it increases the likelihood that the Reviewer will approve it without checking it over. It is better to limit Submit-Review to occasions when the content creator actually needs help. Burton even suggested renaming the Submit option to Request Help to emphasize that this step should be used in special cases.

- If too many people are given the right to review content, users tend to pass the buck or to let someone else take care of it. Knowing that several Reviewers can see the same pending list makes it less likely for any one of them to perform the necessary action. Therefore, not too many people should be given the Reviewer function and those who receive it should be available for a specific reason. For example, someone in the Legal Department might have review rights; a user might submit it because the content creator is seeking guidance about potential legal issues (and is not simply seeking general editorial feedback).

Review List Portlet

Plone has a default portlet which displays a list of all items waiting for review. Generally this is a useful portlet for Admin users to enable because it allows easy access to content in the queue. It will appear as a portlet titled **Review List**. It is not required to use the Review List; the Reviewer could simply go to the URL of the pending content and change the appropriate state from the State drop-down list.

Typically, the portlet lists only three or four content items. Each item to be reviewed is represented with its title and last modification date. The list is sorted by submission date, beginning with the item which has awaited review for the longest amount of time. If you hold the mouse cursor over the title, you will also see the description of the item. The bottom link should go to a URL which should provide a full list of items awaiting review. The URL should resemble something like this and can be bookmarked.

http://www.pendelton.edu/full_review_list

Figure 8.2. Review List Portlet

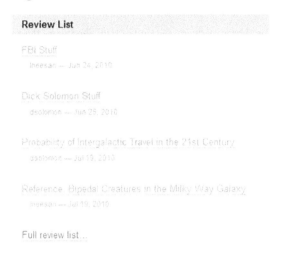

*Click the **Full Review List** link for a more complete listing.*

Making the Approval Decision

When you review a Plone folder or use the **Advanced** state option, you will be presented with additional options about changing the state:

- radio buttons to designate what **state** the item(s) should be.

- **publishing dates and expiration dates**. With both of these, you can enter a date and time. If you enter a publish date, the item will not count as being published until that date at the earliest, even if the "Published" workflow state has already been issued.

- **Comments**. Any notes that the Reviewer makes will appear in the versioning notes. See the section called "Reverting to Previous Saves (History)" [104].

There are two ways to schedule a content item for publication:

- Setting the publishing and/or expiration date for the item on the *Dates* tab when editing it. The content creator can do this.

- Setting these values on the pop-up which appears after the submitter or Reviewer has selected the **Advanced** option on the **State** drop-down menu (on the top right of the Editing bar).

After the item has been submitted, anyone with the Reviewer right would be able to publish and schedule it.

If the expiration date has already passed on the published item, the item will no longer be publicly viewable. If you are logged on, you will see the word "Expired" beside the item's byline. Actually, though, it is easy to extend the expiration date or remove it altogether. The content owner will simply need to edit the item, go to the *Dates* tab, and edit the item's expiration date. After that is done, the content will be published once again; it is not necessary to submit the item again.

Approving Multiple Items Simultaneously

Reviewing and approving content can become tedious if the queue grows too long.

If you visit the URL for the Full Review List, you will see a folder view of all pending content items (Note: these items don't actually exist in the same folder; links to them are simply stored in a single place for convenience). By pressing **Select All** link and choosing **Change State**, you will have the ability to change the state on more items than one.

Figure 8.3. Full Review List

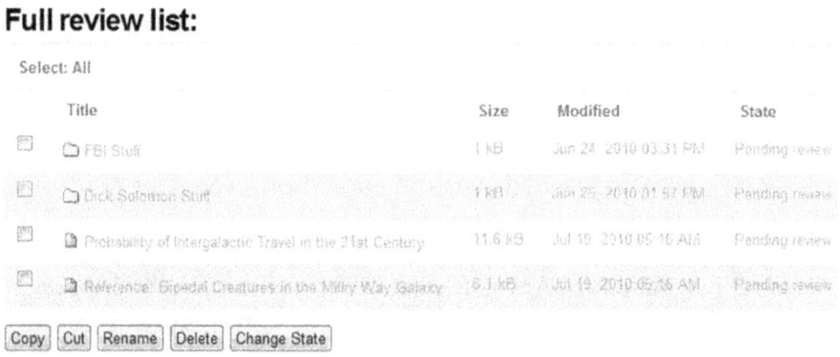

Full review list:

Select: All

	Title	Size	Modified	State
☐	☐ FBI Stuff	1 kB	Jun 24 2010 03:31 PM	Pending review
☐	☐ Dick Solomon Stuff	1 kB	Jun 25 2010 01 57 PM	Pending review
☐	☐ Probability of Intergalactic Travel in the 21st Century	11.6 kB	Jul 15 2010 05 10 AM	Pending review
☐	☐ Reference: Bipedal Creatures in the Milky Way Galaxy	6.1 kB	Jul 14 2010 05:16 AM	Pending review

Copy Cut Rename Delete Change State

Full Review List lets you select several content items at once and to change their state.

In folder view, it is easier to approve multiple content items simultaneously. If you are viewing a folder's contents (by going to a folder and clicking the **Contents** tab), you can check all items in a folder and choosing the Change State button.

Next, you will be presented with a Publishing Process screen which will let you schedule a date for the item(s) to publish. Whenever a folder is on the review list, another option will appear which the Reviewer can check or uncheck "**Include**

contained items." This will cause the status of all the items held within the folders listed there (including subfolders) to be included in the change. If there is no folder in the list, this option will not be available.

In fact, even if you are not at the Full Review List URL, you can use the folder view of any folder to change the state of multiple items. Select the **Contents** tab on a folder, check some or all the content items and then select **Change State**. At that point, you will be presented with the same options as described above.

Republishing Content

The workflow charts in Appendix A, *Basic Plone Workflows* [223] might give the wrong impression that once something is published, it is published for good. In practice, this is not always so clean or easy. More commonly, someone will create an article, submit it, have it approved only to discover a typo. When I post articles online, I'll often edit and re-edit content days – and sometimes even weeks – after something is published. In fact, one might even say that the Internet has radically changed our notion of what publishing really means. In the past, when you produced a print publication, you could not afford to have typos or grammar problems arising too late in the publishing process; printing something again could be expensive or even embarrassing.

Some argue that editorial standards have loosened, or have become more diminished with the advent of web publishing. Whether or not you agree, it is undeniable that the cost of mistakes has also diminished. Suppose you don't catch a typo until after an article is published on the web– not a problem. You can always log back on and correct the typo before anyone notices it. I don't see this capability as making content creators lazy; instead it provides a bigger backstop for catching mistakes during the publication process and beyond.

But this raises questions for the publishing process. How much review should be required? Does an organization want to allow for constant re-editing of content? Or does it want to limit users' abilities to edit content after publication?

Plone expert and trainer Joel Burton once referred to this as the "formal distrust of re-editing." Take the hypothetical case of the CNN editor who takes already published content and inserts something embarrassing or unprofessional in it after it has been approved. If there is a risk in allowing people to reedit their content post-publication, what should an organization do– require that a content item go through another submission & review process each time a typo is corrected? One might hope that the content creator would make an effort to make necessary editorial changes before submission, but in the real world, typos and mistakes are always found even after a person feels 100% sure that an article contains none.

If you require review for all content, you will need to address the case of republishing content. Here are some strategies:

- **Set guidelines for when Reviewers need to review and approve content.** If your editorial department is trying to limit the number of times that an article can be submitted for approval, a rule could be established that allows the article be submitted only once for review–and once approved, it will no longer be available to resubmit. In other words, you are not making Plone require a review for every case; setting guidelines will limit the number of reviews that will be necessary.

- **Obtain a "second pair of eyes" by having the content creator share the document with another person designated to proofread things.** Plone makes it easy to share editorial control of your content with other users. These other users would not be reviewing the content in-depth, but simply participating in the editorial process. Because Plone already has mechanisms to prevent users from editing content simultaneously, as well as the ability to roll back to previous versions, the risk of losing your changes is also minimal. This second pair of eyes would have the role of approving content and assisting the content creator in catching obvious typos before it is submitted for review.

- **Require Submission & Review only in selected folders of the site while allowing users to publish directly on the rest of the site.** More visible areas of the site or more sensitive areas may naturally require tighter controls. This could be accomplished by using a "Submit-is-optional" workflow for the site, while using a different workflow for other specified folders. A user with the manager role can do this by enabling the *Workflow Policy Manager* add-on and configuring a workflow policy for that specific folder. This will be discussed later in this chapter.

If your site requires review, it's a good idea for Reviewers to make sure they know how to use the history link to compare different versions of the same document. One thing which makes reviewing so time consuming is that Reviewers don't know what has changed since the last time they reviewed an item. The Reviewer could use the history tab to compare the latest version with the version he last reviewed (even if the item has already been saved several times since then).

Using Working Copies to edit published items

Plone has a solution to the republishing problem. If the site has enabled the Working Copy feature, a user can check out a temporary private working copy of the published item and edit that while the published item remains untouched. Then, when the user decides that the working copy is polished enough to replace the version currently published, he can check in this copy to replace it. For more information, see the section called "Checking Out Working Copies of Published Items" [107].

Advanced Workflow Topics

Normally, a content creator does not have the power to change workflow for a folder. Changes to workflow will usually be initiated by the Admin User.

Changing Workflows for Individual Folders

Because a site or organization typically has different rules and approval processes, it does not make sense to use the same workflow across the entire site.

There are two ways to handle this:

- Create a custom content type with a different workflow.

- Add a different workflow policy to a folder as the need arises.

Sometimes it makes sense to create a custom content type with a different workflow. This can be accomplished with simple modifications to built-in content types, except specifying a different workflow and a different name for the content type.

Another alternative is to use a workflow policy which applies only for a single folder. This policy is called **Placeful Workflows**, and it must be enabled by a user with the Manager role. You activate this feature by going to **Site Setup --> Add-Ons** and then activating an add-on called **Workflow Policy Support**. This add-on is also known as CMF Placeful Workflows.

Placeful workflow, once activated, puts a configuration screen on Site Setup. It lets the user with the Manager role create new workflows for use in other folders on the site.

Here's a common scenario where you might wish to do this. Suppose your site wants generally to have a loose publishing process, while controlling the access and visibility of certain folders with sensitive content.

To change a folder's workflow:

1. When logged in as a user with the Manager role, go to the folder and choose **Policy** under the **State** drop-down on the right.

2. Click on the **Add a workflow's local configuration** in the folder.

3. Choose the workflow you wish to be in effect for this folder. *Note:* You will need to specify the workflow that applies for the folder itself and for all contents underneath the folder.

After you press Save, a new workflow will be in effect for the folder and its contents.

Notifying People when content has been submitted or published

If you want to be notified when a content item has been submitted and approved, you can use the **Review portlet**. The Review portlet will normally appear to people who have the Reviewer role globally or for a folder.

But what happens if your site is updated infrequently or if you don't normally log in to the site?

Plone has a useful mechanism for sending e-mails automatically, when triggered by a specified action. For example, e-mails could be automatically sent when an item is submitted to a folder, or when a content item is made private or public. These triggering mechanisms are called **content rules**, and they are covered more extensively in the next chapter, Chapter 9, *Using Content Rules* [142]

Chapter 9. Using Content Rules

Admin users can set up triggers which cause Plone to perform certain actions. These triggers are referred to as "content rules." An Admin user creates and configures these content rules via the Content Rules control panel in *Site Setup*. After content rules are set up, they can be added to individual Plone folders.

Why use content rules? Here are some reasons:

- To provide e-mail notifications to content creators when an item has been published or sent back. One way to ensure a smoother (and speedier) publication process is to make sure the creator of a content item is e-mailed when a Reviewer decides to publish or send back something.

- To automatically move content to a different folder when a certain condition has been met. People using Plone are sometimes confused about the correct place on the site to add content. A content rule can simplify this somewhat by allowing an item to be submitted from any place on the site. When it is published, the item will be moved into a more prominent folder (i.e., /blogposts or /editorials or /pressreleases). This kind of content rule works best when the site uses custom content types instead of general ones.

- To keep an administrative log of certain events for troubleshooting and record-keeping.

- To set up e-mail alerts whenever something strange or noteworthy happens (like deleting the home page or deleting a user account).

- To post onscreen messages to a user who completes a certain action.

Many sites manage perfectly fine without using content rules, but content rules can help solve certain kinds of content management problems.

Content Rules for Plone

1 **Triggering Event**
(Also: specify here whether the rule will execute only once or run continuously.)

Options: (Pick Only 1)
Object Added to this Container
Object Modified
Object Removed from Container
User Created/Removed
User Logged In/Out
Workflow State Changed

Conditions
(Will the content rule apply every time a triggering event occurs or only when specific condition(s) have been met for this event?)

Options(Pick 0 or more)
Content Type
File Extension
User's Group
User's Role
TALES Expression
Workflow state
Workflow Transition

2

Actions
(After you choose an option, Plone will prompt you to give more more details.)

Options (Pick 1 or more)
Logger
Notify User
Copy to Folder
Move to Folder
Delete
Transition Workflow State
Send email

3

Assignment
(Which folder(s) will this rule apply to?)

Either:
Rule applies to entire site
Or:
Folder Owner will need to enable the content rule for any folder(s) it should apply to

Although the configuration interface for content rules is easy to use, it may take some practice to make a content rule do what it is supposed to. As the above diagram indicates, content rules involve four components: a triggering event, an optional filtering condition, one or more triggered actions, and assignment of the content rule to one of more folders.

To illustrate how to configure a content rule, we will configure one which e-mails the content creator when a content item has been sent back to the content creator for revision. This is a common scenario and it should illustrate how to configure other kinds of e-mail triggers.

Before starting, here are some things to keep in mind:

1. It's possible to have more than one content rule running simultaneously.

2. It's better to test a content rule on one private folder before you start using it.

3. If your content rule will send an e-mail, make sure that the e-mail actually contains useful information. Ideally, it should be for a unusual or note-worthy event, so you are not drowning users with notification e-mails they will never read.

4. Try to give each content rule a meaningful and descriptive name (using the title and description fields). When you need to assign rules to folders later, you will need to remember what each individual rule does.

5. Depending on which condition or action you have chosen, Plone will let you choose additional related options. The options may differ according to which condition or action you have already selected, but generally their meaning should be clear in the context.

6. TALES Expressions can be used to customize a condition programmatic-ally. It is short for "Template Attribute Language," a special syntax for Zope Page Templates. For more information about using TAL, check the Plone.org website.

To reach the Content Rules control panel, go to **Site Setup --> Content Rules** when logged in as an Admin user. You must verify that the Disabled Globally has *not* been checked. To start, click on the **Add Content Rule** button.

Setting Up the Trigger Event

After you click this button, a **Add Rule** pop-up menu appears. You need to fill out several options.

- **Triggering Event** Please note that after you choose a triggering event you cannot change the event without deleting the rule itself. For this ex-ample, you will choose *Workflow State Changed*.

- **Enabled?** As long as you don't check the option at the bottom of the control panel to *Apply Rule on the Whole Site*, you can check this option since the user will still need to enable the rule manually on folders.

- **Stop Executing Rule?** This rule is mainly used when you plan to have more than one rule simultaneously running on the same folder or the same site, and you don't want any other rules to run when a triggering event has occurred.

For this example, we will call the rule "*Email author when item has been sent back*", enable it and leave blank the option to *Stop evaluating content rules after this rule completes.*

Setting Up Conditions

It is not necessary to specify a condition for every content rule, but in this example, it is important to add a condition.

After you set up the trigger event and push the *Save* button, the pop-up will disappear, and you will return to the main control panel again. You will see your choices reflected onscreen, but you will also see an **Add Content** drop down menu. In this example, the correct option would be *Workflow Transition.* From there, a pop-up window opens to indicate the specific workflow transition condition. In this example, you would choose *Send back.* **Note:** Here you can choose more than one transition by clicking the first item you want, then holding the Control button to select additional workflow states.

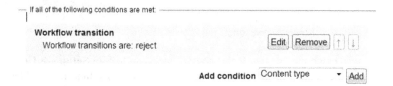

You can select more than one condition for a trigger event.

But why wouldn't you choose the option *Workflow State* instead? Both options sound similar, but they apply to different circumstances. *Workflow Transition* refers to the changing from one state to another, while *workflow state* refers to the final state after being changed. In many cases, either can be selected with the same outcome. But to "send back" and "to retract" will result in the same "private" state. If you choose the workflow state to be private, that will include both the *send back* and *retract* transitions. On the other hand, if you choose the trigger to be *workflow transition* = send back, a user who is retracting his own item won't cause the triggering event.

After you click **Save**, the pop-up will disappear and return you to the main control panel. You will notice that you can edit or remove this condition and also add another condition.

Setting Up Actions

Every content rule needs to have at least one action associated with it. When you choose any option under the drop-down menu for Actions, a pop-up will prompt you to configure more options. For this example, we will be selecting the option *Send email to user*, but before we do that, let's review the other possible actions:

- **Logger**. This will put a message in the system logs for the Plone server. You can customize the Message and include variables which will show certain values in the output: **&e** = the triggering event, **&c** = the context, **&u** = the user. For example, if you add **&e** in the Message field, when the output is printed to the log, you will see the name of the event instead of the variable. Logs can be viewed in several ways. One way is to go to *Site Setup --> Errors*, error_log in the ZMI or on other system files (depending on the setup). Managing logs for the application server lies beyond the scope of this book; suffice to say that this is one way to log certain events.

- **Notify User**. This action will cause a message to appear on a web page after a certain trigger has occurred. For this example, if a user sends back an item in a context where this content rule is running, the user notification will appear to the user in a small message box at the top of the page after performing the action. This action might be useful, for instance, if you wanted to post an informational message about the typical wait time for reviewing to the user who performed the triggering event.

- **Move/Copy/Delete Object**. For move/copy, a pop-up will prompt you to choose the new location for the object.

The *Notify User* action may not sound exciting, but it is a useful default action to experiment with before trying more complex actions. With this simple action, you can verify that a triggering event and conditions have caused a content rule to be invoked. After you are comfortable with these basics, you can change the action to something more sophisticated.

Before we cover the action "Send E-mail," be aware of a few of the common e-mail misconfigurations which might cause a message not to be sent:

- The SMTP Host is not configured. Normally, the SMTP host should already be set up, but this step could be easily overlooked in a test environment.

- The logged-in user may not have an associated e-mail address, or is associated with an inactive e-mail address.

- Sent e-mails may be hidden in the spam folder.

- The content rule may use the wrong substitution for the user's e-mail address.

To solve these basic kinds of errors, it is useful to configure a content rule only for testing. By sending an e-mail containing all the variable substitutions, we can identify what each substitution refers to. This will be covered in the next section.

Now let's look at the configuration pop-up which displays when you choose the *Send e-mail* action.

- **e-mail recipients**. Presumably you would want to use a substitution here. (If you wish to use more than one, put a comma in between). See the next section for details.

- **Exclude actor from recipients**. The label says "Do not send the e-mail to the user that performed the action." If you are a Reviewer and you reject a submission, then regardless of who is supposed to receive a copy of this e-mail, this option will ensure that not be receiving an e-mail notification.

The body text of the e-mail message can contain your text as well as any substitutions. A list of possible substitutions is included in the pop-up below the space where you enter text.

Drafting an Email Notification with Substitutions

Below are the contents of a sample e-mail that you can use as a reference, containing some of the most popular substitutions you may want to use:

Sample Email with Substitutions Use this to test and verify your content rule:

SUBJECT: "${title}" submission has been published

EMAIL RECIPIENTS: ${owner_emails},

MESSAGE:

Your item "${title}" at ${absolute_url} has been published ${effective}. If you need to make revisions after publication, simply change the state from "Published" to "Retract." If you do this, you will need to submit it again after you are finished with your edits.

User's email is: ${user_email} .

user id is: ${user_id}

Contributors' emails are: ${contributor_emails}

Member Email is: ${member_emails}. This refers to all members of a particular website.

Emails of Owners are: ${owner_emails}

Emails of contributors are: ${contributor_emails}

Email of possible editors for this content item are: ${editor_emails}

Email of all users with the reviewer role for this content item are: ${reviewer_emails}

Name of user who created the item, according to the Dublin Core field ${creators}

Transition Title is: ${change_title}

Review State is: ${review_state} Review State Title is: ${review_state_title}

If the Reviewer wrote a comment (after choosing "Advanced' on the drop-down option under State, here it is: ${change_comment}

Now suppose Dick Solomon creates a folder called *Class Projects*, and he gives Tommy Solomon the ability to add a folder (*Laser Tricks*) that he has full ownership rights for. Tommy creates a content item in this folder, and then submits it for publication. Jennifer Ravelli is the Reviewer, and has the right to approve submissions for publication. If the content rule is supposed to send an e-mail to the item creator after it is approved for publication, the following conditions would be met:

- *User_id* will refer to the user who approved the content. In this case, the user is the Reviewer Jennifer Ravelli, and the action of approving the content is the triggering event.

- *${owner_emails}* and *${contributor_emails}* will refer to Dick and Tommy. Even though Dick didn't create or edit the item, he would still be considered a contributor and owner because his ownership & permissions extend recursively from the *Class Projects* folder. **Note:** ${contributors} refers to the Dublin Core field for Creators on the item's *Creator* tab and is completed manually. It has nothing to do with ${contributor_emails} which is derived from the ownership properties of the Plone object.

- In the substitution list, you may notice several variables listed under *Dublin Core*. Dublin Core is an international standard for metadata, but in this context, it refers to several fields on the item's *Creators* tab. Plone will automatically add the user who created the item to the Creators field, but the Creators and Contributors fields on this tab actually have nothing to do with ${owner_emails} or ${contributor_emails} on the variable substitution list.

- *Editor_emails* will refer to all users with editing rights over this content, including users who have been explicitly given that right, and any users with the global role of editor.

- Effective date -- *${effective}* -- will refer to when the item was most recently published.

For this action, the subject line should read: **"${title}" submission has been published** and the recipient line would read: **${owner_emails}**.

Using this example as a model, you can customize the e-mail message as you see fit.

Assigning the Content Rules to a Folder

After you have configured the triggering event and action for a content rule, the final step is to decide which parts of the site the content rule will apply to.

When you add and configure a content rule, you will see a section at the bottom of the page called *Assignments*. It will have a button **Apply Rule on the Whole**

Site. Typically, this option is not checked. Instead, an Admin user will select folders where the content rule(s) will be active.

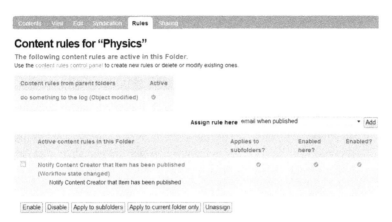

The "Rules" tab lets you add, enable and disable content rules for a folder.

When configuring content rules, it is best to experiment on test content before enabling the rules on your actual live content.

Start off by creating a folder in the private state, and then add your test content there.

Next, click on the **Rules** tab for the folder containing your content. This tab will show you all the content rules currently running in this folder, including those rules which were inherited from higher folders. Make note of the additional options at this point:

- **Assign Rule here**. The drop-down box will list all the content rules which are available.

- **Enable/Disable Buttons**. Disable lets you keep the rule associated with a folder even while it remains inactive. Enable lets you re-enable a rule which was previously disabled.

- **Apply to Subfolders**. Note that you normally would not be able to disable rules which are inherited from parent folders.

- **Apply to Current Folder Only**. You will still be able to add the rule manually to a subfolder, but you will be able to do this one folder at the time.

A rule will not be "enabled" until it has been assigned to at least one folder. To test your content rule, you need to perform the triggering event and then check to see if the expected conditional action has occurred. After you have verified that the content rule works in a private test folder, you can add the rule to other folders and possibly even apply it to subfolders as well.

Final Words: Be Careful!

A parting cautionary anecdote to those using content rules:

While writing this chapter, I observed that after editing an item, my Plone site would exhibit some alarming behavior--the recently edited item would disappear, and then Plone would log me out and display an error message. At first, I thought this may have been a Plone authentication bug, until I realized that I had accident-ally created a content rule which would automatically delete content items after I had edited them. While I hadn't set up that rule on purpose, it took some time to realize that a content rule had been responsible for the deletions. Since content rules work in the background, the only sure way to know what actions are being performed is to check the Rules tab for a folder.

This anecdote illustrates that, even when a content rule is properly configured, if the site is using a large number of rules, their interactions have the potential to do unexpected things. Better testing can detect these kinds of issues, and while most of the time content rules won't be the culprit, you should not rule them out if you're observing inexplicable Plone behavior. Temporarily disabling content rules for a folder, or for the whole site is a quick way of eliminating content rules as the culprit.

Chapter 10. Managing Portlets

One of the best ways of enhancing the usability of a website is to make it easier to navigate. In Plone, a portlet is a web component which is displayed on the left or right side of the primary page content. Although the functions of portlets vary a great deal, most portlets will display supplemental information or have quick links to relevant URLs or user-specific information. For the anonymous visitor, a portlet will appear as a sidebar, or a box on the left or right side of the screen.

General Characteristics of Portlets

Here are some general characteristics of portlets:

- Portlets can be rearranged. In the portlet management interface, it is relatively easy to move one portlet above another, stack several on top of each another, or shift a portlet from the left side to the right side of the page.

- Portlets can show dynamic or static content.

- Portlets can be visible to all viewers, or only to certain users, depending on the rights defined.

- Portlets can be visible in certain sections of the website, but not in others.

- By default, the creator of a content item does not have the right to control what portlet appears with it. For ways to grant limited rights to users so they can configure the portlets that appear, please see the section called "Advanced Topics " [123]).

- Portlets are easy to configure *as long as your user account has the right permissions*. Admin users have the right to add and edit portlets. Although it requires additional customization, it is possible for regular users and group members to be given the right to manage portlets. See the section called "Giving Group Members the rights to manage or add Portlets in certain folders " [126].

For this section, we shall assume that you have some ability to create and/or configure portlets for your content. Even if you don't have rights to configure portlets, it can be helpful to know how portlets are configured and how they can solve common navigation problems.

Accessing the Portlet Manager

If you have the right to manage a portlet, when you browse a web page, you will see a thin, wide, gray rectangular box under all the portlets on the left or right side. Inside this box you will see the words **Manage Portlets**. Clicking this will bring up a screen for configuring portlets.

The available portlets will differ according to the Plone folder you are in. When configuring portlets, you should be aware of your current URL because it indicates which virtual folder(s) are on the page. The series of hyperlinks at the top of the page, usually referred to as *breadcrumbs* or breadcrumb links, will indicate this as well.

When you are in the portlet manager for a folder, you can add different types of portlets: *static text, calendar, classic, collection, search, login, events, RSS feed, news, navigation, review list, recent items.*

Here are some terms used to describe portlets:

- A **Parent Portlet** is simply a portlet which was added at a higher folder. You can block Parent Portlets with the portlet manager even if you did not set it up yourself.

- A **Group Portlet** is a special portlet which pops up if you belong to a specific group. They are configured in Site Setup by the Admin user.

- A **Content-Type Portlet** is a special portlet which appears whenever a visitor is viewing a content item belonging to the specified type. They are configured in Site Setup by the Admin user.

The rest of this chapter will cover how to use each kind of portlet.

Hiding Portlets

If you have the right to manage portlets, you also have the ability to hide portlets. There are two ways to hide a portlet:

1. If the portlet was added at that specific folder, you will have the option to hide the portlet at this level (by clicking the word *Hide* inside the box).

2. If the portlet was added at a higher folder, it will be considered a *parent folder*. If this is the case, you will not be able to hide that specific portlet. The portlet manager also gives you the option to block Parent Portlets by going to the Parent Portlets drop-down list and choosing **Block**.

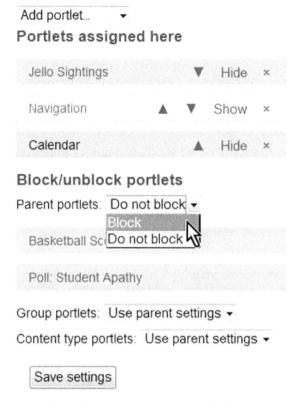

You can block all Parent Portlets, but not individual Parent Portlets.

After a Parent Portlet is blocked at the current level, it will still appear under the list of Parent Portlets.

- Any portlet which has a white background is a blocked (or hidden) portlet.

- Portlets which are blocked at a higher level will not be visible for you to unblock, even if you are the user who originally blocked them at a higher level.

- You have the right to block all Parent Portlets not created by you.

- Even when a portlet has been blocked, you may still have the right to access its configuration screen by clicking on the portlet's name. Generally, you can access the portlet's configuration screen for any portlet you've created, but not for a portlet created by another user.

Which portlets will appear on my web page?

For the rest of this section, we will assume that your user account has the right to add and edit a portlet. Permissions will be covered in the section called "Advanced Topics " [123]. But let's consider a more basic question first: how do you know which portlet(s) appear for a certain URL?

Portlets are added to folders. If you add a portlet high in the Plone folder hierarchy, then the portlet will appear on all its subfolders, unless otherwise specified. If you have the ability to configure portlets for a certain folder, you also have the right to hide (but not delete) portlets already added at a higher place in the folder hierarchy. You also have the right to add/configure a portlet which is more relevant to a specific folder (and subfolders) in a site.

Let's say that we added and subtracted portlets for our imaginary university site, Pendelton State University. We will use the plus and minus signs to indicate the level at which portlets were added and subtracted.

- **Main folder**: + News Portlet (Announcements), + Events Portlet, + Static Portlet (containing graphic of school symbol)

    - **Academics folder** - Events Portlet, +Navigation Portlet, - Static Portlet (containing graphic), + Static Portlet (containing academics graphic)

        - **Physics Department Folder**: -News Portlet (Announcements), - Static Portlet (graphic for academics), + Static Portlet (graphic for Physics Department) +News Portlet (Physics Only), + Collection Portlet (Physics Research Projects)

            - **Physics Home Page** (*what Portlets will appear here on this content item?*)

            - **Dick Solomon Folder**: -Navigation Portlet, -News Portlet (Physics only), -Static Portlet (graphic for Physics Department), - Collection Portlet (Physics Research Project).

                - **Biographical Sketch** (*what Portlets will appear on this content item?*)

Here are the portlets which actually would appear at each level:

- **Main folder**: News Portlet (Announcements), Events Portlet, Static Portlet (containing graphic of school's symbol)

  - **Academics folder** News Portlet (Announcements), Navigation Portlet, Static Portlet (containing an academic graphic)

    - **Physics Department Folder**: Navigation Portlet, Static Portlet (graphic for Physics), News Portlet (Physics Research Project)

      - **Physics Home Page** (*what Portlets will appear here on this content item?*)

    - **Dick Solomon Folder**: Nothing!

      - **Biographical Sketch** (*what Portlets will appear on this content item?*)

Portlets are configured for folders, but they appear on content items (mainly pages). Basically, the Portlets that appear on a content item will be the same as those configured to appear in the folder (where the content item is contained). The example above lists two content items. They will contain *exactly the same* Portlets as the folder containing them. So the result will be:

Physics Home Page: Navigation Portlet, Static Portlet (graphic for Physics), News Portlet (Physics Research Project)

...

Biographical Sketch: Nothing!

A few notes on the above example:

So far, we've assumed that none of the Portlets added were content-type Portlets or Group Portlets. Content-type Portlets don't need to be added to a specific folder, but instead, they appear whenever a certain content type is being viewed. Group Portlets are tied to the user, not a folder or a content type, and they appear whenever a member of a specified group has logged on. These kinds of Portlets will appear globally, but can be blocked from view for specific folders (and subfolders).

Second, the example demonstrates that it is not always clear if you are viewing a folder's content, an autogenerated collection, or a manually created page. Every folder has a default view, and it is common for folder owners to designate a single content item as the default view. That can be confusing when you are trying to calculate which Portlet should appear.

Third, this example illustrates how varied the number of Portlets displayed for each level can be. Portlets can offer a lot of customization, and if content-type

Portlets and Group Portlets were also used in this example, you would have even more customization.

Fourth, in this example, all the Portlets were turned off in Dick Solomon folder. Turning off Portlets for certain folders can be a good thing, since Portlets are distracting. If you turn off all the Portlets for one or both sides, you widen the viewing area for the content to be displayed. This can be ideal for personal pages for example. Also, turning off Portlets for certain folders prevents the site as a whole from having a "cookie-cutter feel."

Using the Portlet configuration screen

Before we discuss how to configure each different type of Portlet, let's go over the basic interface.

Remember: The Portlets visible on the Manage Portlets menu will depend on the folder you are in, and which Portlets have been configured above the current folder.

Now let's review the options available on the Portlet configuration screen:

- The **Add Portlet** option will contain a list of Portlets which you have the right to add in this folder. After you choose one, a dialogue will appear which allows you to configure the Portlet. **Note:** There are two Add Portlet buttons – one for the left side and one for the right.

- The **Portlets Assigned Here** option will contain a graphical list of Portlets added and configured for the current folder and below. That does not include any Portlets which were created above this folder which are now visible. If there are no grey boxes immediately below this section, it means no Portlets have yet been added. After you add a Portlet in the current folder, you will see a gray rectangle corresponding to the Portlet you just added.

- The **Block/Unblock Portlets** option will show a list of all Parent Portlets created at higher folders, which now appear in the current folder. Active and unblocked Portlets will appear as gray rectangles directly underneath this section. The color of the text within the grey rectangle indicates whether the Portlet can be configured or not:

  - If the text font inside the grey Portlet rectangle is **blue**, you have the right to configure this Portlet.

  - If the text font inside the grey Portlet rectangle is **black**, you do *not* have the right to configure this Portlet. Even though you cannot edit the Portlet, you still will have the right to block them from view.

- **Group Portlets** This section of the Portlet configuration screen lets you choose whether to block or show any Portlets displayed for a particular group. The default selection is *Use Parent Setting*, and that is generally a safe choice. If your site uses Group Portlets, they are generally applicable to group members throughout the site and not just in one section.

  Example: Suppose there is a group called *Faculty* and the Admin user creates a new Portlet to display a meeting announcement whenever a faculty member logs on. Although Group Portlets are created and maintained by the Admin user, anyone with access to the *Manage Portlets* screen can actually disable them for a folder and its subfolders. In this example, a user in the physics department with access to Portlet management could block this new Faculty Portlet from appearing. Remember that this Portlet won't actually appear in the Physics folder and subfolders, but it will still appear as a possible Portlet under Group Portlets which could then be blocked or unblocked. If Dick Solomon has permissions to manage Portlets in his own folder (physics/Dick Solomon Stuff), he could simply unblock the Faculty Group Portlet so that it appears whenever he is looking at items inside his own folder.

- **Content-Type Portlets** are Portlets configured by the Admin user which are associated with a specific content type instead of a folder. For example, the Admin user may decide that every time a visitor goes to an Event content item that a Portlet of a calendar graphic should also appear. This Portlet will be added to every default view of Events, regardless of where the visitor is browsing on the site. The Portlet manager also allows you to hide Content-Type Portlets with three options:

  - **Use parent settings** *(default)*. This just means to obey whatever was configured for a higher folder. If a Content-Type Portlet was enabled for root level, but disabled for second level, then if you had this for the third level, the Content-Type Portlets would be hidden for this level as well.

  - **Block**. This lets you block Content-Type Portlets which by default would appear alongside a certain item type.

  - **Do Not Block**. This is only used when the site uses Content-Type Portlet(s) and the Portlet has been blocked by a parent folder. Choosing *Do Not Block* will toggle Content-Type Portlets so they will resume appearing for content in this folder and subfolders.

Because Content-Type Portlets apply globally and because they override what you configure in the Portlet manager, they are rarely used. Here are some situations where Content-Type Portlets *might* be used:

- A Portlet can have help information related to a specific content type.

- Your site uses a different or nonstandard content type which might require some identifying logo or announcement related to the content type.

- An event type (for example) might include a calendar graphic in a Portlet whenever an event is shown.

If you block every Portlet on a side, the column which normally contains the Portlet will disappear and will widen the overall width of the main content area.

When experimenting with Portlets, it is a good idea to keep two or more browser windows open. One should remain open to the Manage Portlets screen, and the other should remain open to the folder URL. You can also use a different browser to view the folder as an anonymous visitor.

Ordering and Rearranging Portlets

Plone gives you the ability to rearrange Portlets.

In the **Portlets Assigned Here** subsection, there are four available actions for each Portlet:

- **Clicking on the Portlet name in blue text** inside the gray Portlet box will bring you to the configuration screen for editing.

- **Clicking on the word "Hide" in blue text inside the gray box** allows you temporarily hide or show a *Portlets Assigned Here* Portlet. After it is hidden, the gray box will turn white and the word will change to **Show**.

- **Clicking on the X inside the gray box** will automatically kill your Portlet without prompting you for a confirmation. *Don't do this unless you are absolutely sure you want to do this!* Sure, you can probably add the Portlet again, but it's likely that you may not remember all the settings you used previously. It is much safer to hide a Portlet than to kill it. Kill a Portlet only after you are certain that you do not need it and never will again.

- **Clicking the up triangle or down triangle** will change the order of the respective Portlets as they will appear in the browser. Note that this changes the order only of the Portlets listed in the *Portlets Assigned here* subsection. The Portlet Manager does not allow you to move a Portlet in *Portlets Assigned Here* to underneath a Group Portlet or a Parent Portlet.

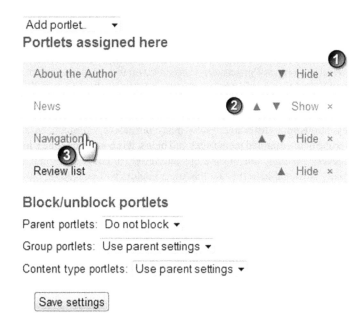

1. Clicking the X will permanently delete any Portlet. 2. The Hide/Show toggle lets you change a Portlet's visibility. Here, the News Portlet has been hidden. 3. Portlets that have additional configuration screens will have names which are hyperlinks. When you hover over its name, the cursor will change to a hand.

Be sure to press the **Save Settings** button after you make any configuration change to the Portlets, or your changes will not take effect.

By default, Plone places any Portlets which you added specifically for this folder (in the *Portlets Assigned Here* section) higher than any Portlets inherited from higher folders. You cannot reorder inherited Portlets over your own folders. This limitation is logical, since you would typically want Portlets which are more relevant to your specific content to be placed more prominently than generic sitewide Portlets, which are less likely to apply directly to you. For example, if you are at a folder for the Physics department, a Portlet for the physics department is probably more relevant than a general Portlet for the larger university site.

Remember: Do not click the X on *Portlets Assigned Here* section unless you want to permanently kill it! Hiding a Portlet is generally safer.

Left or Right? Both or Neither?

The next question is which side of the web site should you put your Portlet? How many Portlets is too many?

When trying to decide on which side to add a Portlet, it's best to follow the conventions for the rest of the site. As a general rule, navigation and functional Portlets (i.e., review Portlets, etc.) should go on the left side of the page. Portlets that offer additional information or additional links should go on the right side. This is just a convention, however, and nothing is sacrosanct about this placement.

Conventions may differ about how many portlets is too much. In the world of advertisement-saturated media sites and blogs, it is common to see a lot of content widgets on the right side of the page, and fewer (or none) on the left side. This is partially attributable to the fact that most visitors will be reading the pages from left to right, and the widgets are placed to take advantage of most visitors' natural reading patterns. Alternatively, for blog sites with vertically lengthy pages, numerous widgets on the right side will not stand out as prominently. Depending on the design of your Plone site, you may want to shrink the size of the portlets on either side, or block all the portlets on a side entirely.

Blocking all the portlets for the left or right section has the advantage or opening up more white space and freeing up width for the primary content. This can be good or bad, depending on your needs. While more white space may not be as visually appealing, it has also been found to improve comprehension. Having the extra space is also useful if the page needs to accomodate an oversized graphic, or a table with many columns.

The answer may depend partially on the design decisions made by your site's web designer. Your web designer might have specified a minimum width for all three columns (in which case, expanding the space for the main content might actually look bad). Once again, you should look at other areas of the site and see what the conventions are.

The web designer will probably test the look of a site in various dimensions and devices. Evolving CSS standards (and in particular, CSS Media Queries) now makes it relatively easy for a URL to drop out columns when viewed on smaller mobile devices.

How wide should a web page be?

Generally, your site's web designer has to decide the optimal layout of columns and the maximum width of your primary content area. When trying to decide whether you need portlets on both sides or only one side, you should keep this research in mind:

- The rule of thumb from many web typography books is that the optimal number of characters per line is 55 to 75. In reality, it is common to see anywhere between 75 and 90 characters per line on a web page. It is also no longer unusual for some sites to have more than 100 characters per line.

- A study (Lin, 2004) found that good use of white space between paragraphs and in the left and right margins increases comprehension by nearly 20%. Readers find it easier to focus on and process generously spaced content.

- 96% of websites do not justify text.

Source: Smashing Magazine, 2009. http://bit.ly/12OjfT

Which portlet should you use?

The rest of the chapter will contain descriptions of all the available portlets you can add. Most of the time you will only need two portlets: collection portlets and static text portlets. Recently, Plone improved its interface for configuring collections; now it is extremely easy to configure and invoke them in a collection portlet. I recommend trying to use a collection portlet before you try anything else. Navigation portlets can help when you want folders to appear in search results. Review portlets are convenient things for users who need to review content. Static text portlets are helpful for displaying small graphics (like ads, etc.) Group portlets are helpful for creating customized dashboards for different groups of users.

Static Text Portlets

Static Text portlets are the most straightforward.

Portlet header	Title of the rendered portlet. (It will also be displayed to identify the portlet in the Portlet Manager). This is a required field, so it will automatically show at the top of the portlet unless you have chosen Omit Portlet Border. *(Required)*

Text space	Adding content through TinyMCE. If you include an image, be sure to modify the image's settings to choose an appropriate size. Plone will not automatically reduce the size for you. Depending on the site's CSS, the portlet column may expand if you have not reduced the image. *(Required)*
Omit Portlet Border	Checking this will remove the gray header and footer and show only the body text of the static Portlet.
Portlet Footer	Text to be shown at the bottom (footer) of the portlet window.
Details Link	If given, the header and footer will link to this URL. If you leave this blank, then the text you enter in the portlet footer will not be a hyperlink. **Note**: Only internal links can be added here. External URLs will not resolve correctly.

Collection Portlets

A collection portlet is a portlet which contains the results of a collection. See the section called "Collections" [94]. Generally only Admin users have the right to create and configure collection portlets, but you can use a collection which someone else has created. Keep in mind that if another user has created a collection, it's theoretically possible for that same user to modify it later.

If you have already created a collection, configuring a portlet for it is fairly easy. The only tricky part is being able to locate the target collection. To do that, you need to know the name (or, to be more precise, the title) of the collection you wish to use.

To associate a collection with a collection portlet:

1. Write down for yourself the name or title of the collection you wish to use.

2. Click the gray **Manage Portlets** button on the bottom of the screen.

3. Choose **Collection Portlet** under the the Add Portlet drop-down menu.

4. Type something in the **Portlet Header** field. **Note**: Whatever you type here will appear at the top of the portlet when visitors see it on the site.

5. Under **Target Collection**, check to see if the collection you wish to associate is already listed in search results. If you already see it listed, simply, check it and configure the rest of the portlet as you normally would.

6. If the collection you wish to associate is not listed, type one or two words from the title and click **Search**.

7. After you see your collection appear underneath as a search result, click the circle beside it and press the **Update** button.

The other options for collections are self-explanatory.

If a collection portlet displays items which are private or pending, they will not be colored red or orange. Instead, the links will appear in the normal blue color even though the items are not yet published.

RSS Portlets

The RSS Portlet is primarily intended to display external feeds. However, it can also display feeds from your own site. *(For more information about generating RSS feeds in Plone, see the section called the section called "Making and Customizing Web Feeds" [195]).*

After you learn the exact URL for the RSS feed, you can add/configure the RSS portlet. On the **Add Portlet** drop-down menu, choose **RSS feed**. You will then be presented with the following options:

Title	Title of the portlet. If omitted, the title of the feed will be used.
Number of Items to Display	How many items to list. *(Required)*
URL of RSS feed	Link of the RSS feed to display.*(Required)* Note: if you have entered the RSS feed improperly, the RSS portlet will not show up on the public website at all, although you will still see the portlet as a gray box on the *Manage Portlets* area.
Feed Reload Timeout	Time in minutes after which the feed should be reloaded. Generally you should use the defaults unless there is a reason to check more often. Keep in mind that if you are checking a popular RSS feed from a smaller site frequently you may be using unnecessary bandwidth. *(Required)*

Review Portlets

A Review list is a list of contents which have been submitted and are waiting for someone to review and to move its status from Pending to Published.

This portlet will only be seen by people who have been given the Reviewer role across the site. For the rest, this portlet will not appear.

There are no options to configure. If this portlet seems intrusive to you, you can hide it and just bookmark the page it links to at **http://www.pendelton.edu/full_review_list** . This URL will generally show all pending content items awaiting review for you.

The review portlet will show all content waiting to be reviewed. That means that it will show both submissions by users as well as commenters (if commenting is enabled). Plone has a separate dashboard for reviewers who are also Admin users to review comments. To access this dashboard, click your user name (at top right of the browser), and choose **Moderate Comments** from the drop-down menu.

Because comments are a separate content type, you could also create a collection portlet which lists all pending comments for a group with the Reviewer role.

In general, it is **recommended** to have a review portlet enabled for the site.

Group Portlets

A Group Portlet (like Content-Type Portlets) is another kind of portlet whose appearance doesn't depend on which folder it's in. Only members of a certain group can view this portlet. Still, any user with the ability to manage portlets for a folder will have the rights to see all the Group Portlets in effect for that location and to block them. Group Portlets always appear below any other active Portlets in a given folder.

Here are the steps for configuring a Group Portlet. You have to be an Admin user to do this.

1. Go to *Site Setup* and choose the **Users and Groups** control panel.

2. Switch to the **Group** tab on the toolbar.

3. Click on the group name you want.

4. Click the **Group Portlets** tab.

From here, you will see the usual portlet configuration screen.

Suppose you were a professor at the university and belonged to a Plone group called Faculty. An Admin user could set up a portlet specifically for Faculty (which would appear throughout the entire site). This Group Portlet could contain information about paychecks, deadlines, benefits, university faculty senate announcements.

This kind of portlet could also be helpful for providing help on the website. Perhaps the Admin user could create a group called Novices which all users would initially belong to (for a period of a week or a month). During this time, portlets could provide useful tips about how to use the Plone site.

Recent Items Portlet

A Recent Items Portlet will show a number of configurable links to recently modified items. These items are not filtered by the user who modified them. This configuration menu consists of only one field, **Number of Items to Display**. Here are some things to keep in mind:

- This portlet shows all items published across the site (rather than only those from a single folder or a single type).

- When a user logs in, he will generally be able to see unpublished items along with published items. (The Admin user can set a sitewide policy of disallowing private/pending/draft documents from appearing to other users in this kind of portlet on the Navigation options in Site Setup. See the section called "Navigation " [206]. There is a URL which lists all recent items at **http://www.pendelton.edu/recently_modified**.

- The only way to exclude certain items from appearing in the Recent Items portlet is to exclude the item altogether from appearing in navigation and searches. See the section called "Exclude certain items from appearing in navigation or searches" [182].

In almost all cases, it is better to configure a collection and collection portlet which can perform the same function (and filter results using another search term or criteria.

Navigation Portlets

Navigation Portlets are powerful tools that can help users jump to nearby places in the site easily. Sometimes a new install may include a navigation portlet pre-configured already. If configured correctly, a navigation portlet will show folders and items which are adjacent to whatever location you happen to be. Keep in mind that the contents of a navigation portlet can also change depending on which content item you are visiting.

Limitations of Navigation Portlets

Although navigation porlets are very useful, and are intended to help navigate the site, they can also be difficult to configure, and have some limitations. Here are a few:

- You cannot set a maximum number of items which appear in the portlet.

- You have limited control over the ordering of these items appearing in the portlet.

- The content appearing in navigation portlets can vary depending on which location it was configured in.

In *Site Setup --> Navigation*, the Admin user can tweak other things related to Navigation portlets:

- Which item types are allowed to appear in the navigation portlet?

- What workflow state must a content item be to appear in the navigation portlet? (Typically, the content creator would want only published items to appear here).

I recommend trying some other solution to the problem; perhaps you can create a collection portlet where the collection lets you fine-tune the items appearing in the portlet. You could also create a simple static portlet that appears only in one or two folders and you could manually add the hyperlinks and folder icon. That might turn out to be easier than configuring and testing a navigation portlet. Next, we will describe two scenarios where navigation portlets can achieve a focused goal.

Two Scenarios for Creating Navigation Portlets

To demonstrate navigation portlets, we shall use the same folder hierarchy as the previous example.

- **Plone Root** :

  - **Academics folder**

    - **Anthropology Department Folder**

    - **English Department Folder**

- **Physics Department Folder**:

  - **Physics Home Page**

  - **(lots of pages)**

  - **Dick Solomon Folder**:

    - **Biographical Sketch**

Scenario One: Show Subfolders from a single level inside a folder

Navigation portlets are useful for showing you the folders that are siblings of your current location's parent folder, but if the folder itself contains content other than subfolders (pages, events, etc), the results are significantly less pretty. First, we'll examine a navigation portlet which we will set up for content inside the Dick Solomon Folder. Since the Academic folder contains only subfolders and we want these subfolders to show up in the portlet, this configuration should work neatly. To start, first check these settings:

- **Root Node**: Choose a folder between the Plone root. For this example, we will choose **Academics**. (Choosing a folder right below the top folder of the Plone site is generally a good idea).

- **Include Top Node**. **Yes**. The Academics folder will always be shown, regardless of where you are on the site. To clarify, this is not site-wide, but within the topmost folder for which the Navigation Portlet was created. In the example, a Navigation Portlet created in the Academics folder and set to Include Top Node will appear within every subfolder of the Academics folder and include a link to the parent Academics folder. Generally a good thing.

- **Only show the contents of the current folder**. Choose **No**.

- **Start Level**: Choose 1.

- **Navigation Tree Depth**. Choose **0**. (That means unlimited amount of folders If you have an extreme number of folders inside the root node Academics, you probably should set a maximum number of 10 or 15).

This will only work if: You have zero or a very small amount of items in the folder you are currently located in. If that is the case, you can block it for that level and unblock it at the next lower level.

Scenario Two: Showing Other Items in the Same Folder

Suppose you want the visitor to have easy access to other items in the same Dick Solomon folder without having to navigate up one level to see the content items. Here's how to do that:

- **Root Node:** Choose the same folder you are in. In this case, it will be **Dick Solomon folder**.

- **Include Top Node. Yes**. The Dick Solomon folder will always be shown, regardless of where you are on the site. Generally a good thing.

- **Only show the contents of the current folder.** Choose **Yes**.

- **Start Level:** Choose **0**.

- **Navigation Tree Depth.** Choose **0**. (The value here is completely overridden by what you chose in *Only Show the Contents of the Current Folder*).

One limitation of this scenario is that you cannot limit the number of items which show up in this portlet. If Dick Solomon folder had 100 items, all 100 would show up.

Navigation Portlet Options

Here is a description of options for the navigation portlet.

Title

The title of the navigation tree. This will be visible to users, but it will *not* be visible in the Manage Portlets screen.

Root Node

You may search for and choose a folder to act as the root of the navigation tree. Leave blank to use the Plone site root. You should **not** leave it blank. It is almost never necessary to create a navigation portlet which will appear at the top level (for example, **www.pendeltonstate.edu** or **www.pendeltonstate.edu/academics**) because often the folders directly below root are already available as tabs on the top of the page.

Include top node

Whether or not to show the top, or 'root', node in the navigation tree. This is affected by the 'Start level' setting. Generally it is

	good to keep this checked. The top node is relative to the folder in which the portlet is added. In any subfolder within the folder in which the portlet is added, a link to the parent folder will appear.
Only show the contents of the current folder.	*If selected, the navigation tree will only show the current folder and its children at all times.* Select this only if you wish the portlet to display *all* the content items inside your current folder. If you check this, the value in navigation tree depth will be overridden, and the portlet will not show any sibling folders. The only folders you see will be subfolders inside the current folder.
Start Level	*An integer value that specifies the number of folder levels below the chosen site root that must be exceeded before the navigation tree will display. A value of "0" means that the navigation tree should be displayed everywhere including pages in the root of the site. A value of "1" means the tree only shows up inside folders located in the root and downwards, never showing at the top level.*
Navigation Tree Depth	*How many folders should be included before the navigation tree stops? 0 means no limit. 1 only includes the root folder.*

Easier Option: Use Static or Collection Portlets Instead

Navigation portlets are complicated to set up, but don't fret it too much. By comparison, it is much easier to create a collection and show the results in a collection portlet or create a static text portlet containing only the links you need.

Calendar Portlets

The Calendar Portlet is linked to events which have been published. It has no configurable options. To configure the Calendar Portlet, go to Site Setup --> Calendar.

After you create a calendar portlet, you will see a miniature calendar inside the portlet showing the current month. Users can easily click the back and forward buttons on the calendar to see what days of the week a date might be or when a scheduled event is.

Figure 10.1. Calendar Portlet

«			August 2010			»
Su	Mo	Tu	We	Th	Fr	Sa
1	2	3	4	5	6	7
8	9	10	11	12	13	14
15	16	17	18	19	20	21
22	23	24	25	26	27	28
29	30	31				

Aug 30, 2010 00:00-02:00 August Midnight Stargazing Bash

Events are hyperlinks on the calendar portlet. Tooltips provide details.

If a published event occurs on one of the days on the calendar, the day will be hyperlinked, and if you hover your mouse on the date's number, you will see a short tooltip explaining what the event is about. If you click on the hyperlink, you will see a link to a list of events which includes the one on the date you selected.

You could achieve this same functionality without the calendar icon by creating a collection of recent events, and then creating a collection portlet which uses this collection.

News Portlets

A news portlet will show a list of links to recent news items. "News items" are a built-in content type. After you create one, select how many news items you wish to appear in the portlet and whether the portlet should only contain published news items, or news items which haven't yet been published. If you want the portlet to include news items which are private/internally published/pending review, you will need to select multiple items by keeping the Control key held down while you select more than one item with your mouse.

Other Portlets

In addition to the portlets described above, there are also: **search portlet** (which shows a search box), **event portlets** (which show upcoming events) and **classic portlet** (used for legacy reasons only). Classic Portlets require a template and macro to be set up, and will display with an error if both are not supplied.

Chapter 11. Improving Navigation & Findability

This chapter will cover the best practices for improving your site organization and making content easy to find. We will discuss:

- The basic principles of findability and information architecture, as they relate to Plone.

- Recommendations for improving the navigation and findability of a Plone site using out-of-the-box features, although the Admin user or site planner may use add-ons and customizations to improve performance further.

- How to use the Search and Advanced Search features.

While many of these recommendations can be implemented by contributors with no special permissions, some of these recommendations will require advanced security permissions, and will be labeled as such.

Findability and Usability

What is findability? It can mean many things, but when we use the term, we are referring to three things:

1. The ability for a user at the site to find a particular piece of content.

2. The ability of a random web surfer to find that piece of content in search results.

3. The ability of a content creator to use a site effectively.

The last sense of the word cannot be overstated. If the content creator does not understand the overall organization of the site, or is unsure about the appropriate way to create content, findability will likely be diminished for all users. In other words, if the content creator doesn't understand the organization of the site, what are the chances that another user would?

A successful user experience on your site does not depend solely on the content management system you have, but it can also depend on a variety of human factors and preferences, many of which are beyond the ability of this book to address. For example, font size would be more important to findability in sites geared toward senior citizens, or those with vision impairments. Many of these factors will fall to your web designer to modify the Plone style sheets on the site and optimize the presentation for your audience. What the content creator should focus on is organizing content so that it is easily findable–and this is a desirable quality in any site.

When thinking about findability, here are some generic questions that CMS contributors should ask:

1. **Can the user easily search for content using the search box?** This question raises the importance of the summary field, especially if you are searching for files (PDFs, DOCs, etc) which are not displayed on the site itself. The Site Administrator also has the right to omit certain item types from appearing in search results, which can help remove unwanted clutter from lists of items. For example, it is common practice to remove the image content type from searches.

2. **If the user doesn't use the search box, would they still be able to find content easily?** If the answer to this question is "no", it could indicate that the top sections of the site are not well-organized or intuitive. Take a university website as an example. The visitors to a university site fall into various categories: parents, students, staff, alumni, etc. Visitors from these groups will be seeking different kinds of content, and will expect their content to be organized in a different way. Parents are going to want to reach financial aid & admissions, students will want to reach current events and student activities, alumni will want to access alumni events and reunion schedules, etc. For this reason, it is acceptable for the structure of each top level folder to be organized differently.

3. **How many clicks are necessary to browse to the appropriate content item?** If there are too many steps (i.e. clicks) to get to your desired content, it could indicate that your folder hierarchy is too deep and should be flattened. Portlets can also reduce the number of clicks needed to reach an item, as well as tags.

4. **Are labels for certain content items ambiguous or confusing for the user?** If the answer to this question is "yes", the content creator should try to create titles and summaries which are unique to those content items, and are helpful in describing them.

5. **When browsing through the site to find things, does the user overlook a link to the item in question?** If the answer to this question is "yes", there are many possible ways to address the problem. It could indicate that items are not well-labelled, that items are overlooked because the page is too long, or that a collection returns too many results. Another possibility is that your collections and folders have not been ordered or arranged properly. See the section called "Rearranging the default order of items in a folder view" [91]. With collections you can set a different

sort order, and with individual folders, you can change the order of items so that the more important ones appear on top.

6. **Is it easy to find similar items?** Diligent and consistent use of tags can make it easier to find similar content that exists in different folders.

7. **Are site security problems getting in the way? Are visitors stumbling onto URLs which they don't have the right to view?** Security problems are not something the content creator normally needs to deal with. Generally though, these kinds of error messages are produced when a folder has not yet been published.

How do you determine whether site visitors are having these kinds of problems? One approach is to find a few users who have no direct or previous knowledge of your site, and give them a series of tasks to perform while you sit beside them. The results can be surprising and instructive. For the Pendelton State University example, you could ask:

1. How would we find the Physics department home page?

2. What classes will Mary Albright be teaching in the fall semester?

3. How do you register for a class?

4. Who do you contact if you want to play intramural sports at the university?

5. Where do I find information about the university lecture series?

Non-hierarchical Content

Content creators on Plone should avoid making the folder structure too deep. Although visitors can use the hyperlink breadcrumbs to ascend through the folder structure, it should not be necessary for site visitors to sort through too many folders, or memorize the folder hierarchy to find what is needed.

Content does not fit neatly inside neat and discrete folders. Consider how a college physics department might be organized:

Physics Department
  Faculty
    Dr. Dick Solomon
      C.V.
      Research Interests
      Class Schedule
    Dr. Vincent Strudwick
      C.V.

       Research Interests
         Papers
       Class Activities
         Field Trip
       Class Wiki (for current students only)
           Introduction to Astrophysics
           Geophysics and Climate Change
       Data Sets for Downloading

   Research
   Policies
   In the News
   Department Events
   Classes
   Visiting Lectures

We can see that faculty members will probably have similar kinds of content underneath their name. But consider the following scenarios:

1. What happens if a content item appropriately belongs to more than one category? For example, what if Vincent Strudwick and Dick Solomon were teaching a class together?

2. What happens if a content item does not belong to any of the existing physics categories, but still is interesting to the physics department? For example, what if the physics student had started an intramural ping pong team?

3. What happens if there is an alternate but equally valid way of organizing the same content? In other words, how do you decide between organizing content chronologically, alphabetically, by user rating, or by any other desired factor?

4. How do you make sure that certain content items are given more prominence than others? For example, if the physics department were planning a symposium, it may want the symposium event to be displayed more prominently than other university events.

Plone has several ways to address these situations. First, you can create queries, called "Collections", that will appear on a certain URL (such as, "Show all Academic Papers on Climate Change between 2007 and 2010 by Pendelton professors"). It is even possible for a Plone developer to create a template to display results from this collection in an easy-to-read fashion. Some examples might include: "Show all Academic Papers on Climate Change and Sort by Professor's Last Name" or "Show all Content on Climate Change but exclude events and lectures."

When you create content, you are also given the option to write in tags, or to pick from a selected list of tags. See the section called "Categorization Component " [61]. You don't need tags to make a collection, but tags do make it easier to create a collection targeted to a specific subject. This can make your content more helpful and relevant to the reader, and more easily discovered.

Even with training, it may be take some time before members of your organization use tags and summaries consistently and effectively. This is partly due to the fact that there are a variety of valid approaches for finding the same information. You should make sure your tags are relevant and understandable, but not overly specific, or overly generic. You should also avoid choosing too many, or too few tags. In other words, the best approach for your needs becomes clear only with time and experience.

Tips for Improving Findability: A Checklist

Use boring but descriptive titles.

Überblogger Cory Doctorow once said that a primary reason his *Boing Boing* blog became so popular was that it used "boring but descriptive headlines." This is not to say that cleverness in your titles should be avoided, but a reminder that titles should ultimately deliver information about your page so it can be found in a search. For this reason, Search Engine Optimization (SEO) is a constant goal for content managers and marketers. It also can be a constantly moving target since Google, Microsoft and other search engine providers are constantly revising their search algorithms. While the content manager should dedicate time to optimizing a site for search, SEO can also be a neverending exercise that will eventually produce diminishing returns for the time spent. While you could always enlist the services of a company dedicated to SEO, we believe using concise, descriptive titles will do wonders for your findability. More importantly, it will save you time and money down the line.

Always add something to the Summary field (and make it different from the title)

The summary field, like the title of a page, will also help to identify what a content item is about. Each page has a field called "Summary" which allows you to describe more fully what the content item contains. Information in this field serves multiple purposes:

1. The summary will appear on the search results page or in a dynamically generated list of content items, such as in a collection. The complete text will be shown.

2. The summary will appear in the meta section of the HTML code

```
<meta content="Dick Solomon's predictions about
intergalactic space travel." name="description"
/>
```

3. The summary will appear under the search box when you type in a term related to it.

4. The summary will appear as the description of a page when creating an internal link. As content grows in number, many items will have similar-sounding titles. Sometimes, the only way to tell the difference between two different pages is the summary description.

The summary field uses a text box with the potential to hold up to 6 lines of text. But that doesn't mean you should try to use all of them. Generally, search engines will only use 160-200 characters in search results while the summary appearing under the search box in your own site will show maybe 95 characters. Although it's not always possible for a summary to convey a page's content, you should at least try to have some of the most important words appear in the initial portion of the summary.

Train users to use internal links correctly

By now many content creators have figured out how to use rich text editors to hyperlink content. The CMS interface usually makes this easy...perhaps too easy.

Linkrot is the tendency for Internet links to break after a certain period of time, and it is a perennial problem. While you cannot control whether the URLs to external, third-party sites go bad, Plone has a way to monitor whether internal links (i.e., links to other parts of the same site) are still valid.

When content creators use the rich text editor, they are given a choice about whether to create an external link or an internal link. In previous versions of Plone, it was simpler for content creators just to paste the full URL, regardless of whether the URL was an internal link or an external one. Now, the editor interface in Plone has been designed specifically to encourage content creators to make internal links.

Internal links also protect you if the site is reorganized and the content is moved into different folders. Using internal links, Plone makes this a seamless transition. If an internal link has been correctly added, Plone will redirect the viewer from the expired URL to the more recent URL. A page link may still use the original URL, but Plone will know to forward it to the right one. From the perspective of system maintenance, using internal links whenever possible substantially reduces the amount of linkrot.

Use Related Items

Plone content types usually have a built-in field for storing related links. To do this, edit your content item and choose the **Categorization** tab. Midway down is a heading for *Related Items*. From there you can add one or more internal links which will appear at the bottom of the published web page.

Use tags effectively

Plone lets you add metadata to almost any content item. In general, the more metadata you can add to your content item, the better. Probably the most important field is the Tag field under the Categorization tab.

Why should the use of tags be encouraged for content items? Tags give readers an additional method for searching and navigating through content. There is a tendency to make Plone sites more hierarchical than they need to be; for that reason, it is necessary to create alternate "sideways" paths for browsing through content. Tags are one way to do this. As long as tags are meaningful and useful and not overused, they can help with navigation.

Make content creators aware of how to use and add tags

Because the tags field is hidden in the second tab marked "Categorization," this step can be easy to overlook. A new content creator might not realize that these options exist or that they need to be filled out. Or a content creator who knew this may have simply forgotten.

It is beneficial for sites to have consistency in how tags are applied to content items, and how they are named. For example, if one contributor applies 5 tags per content item and another contributor never uses them, it will make the tagged content items easier to find than the untagged ones, which may go overlooked. There should also be a consistency in the way tags are named when written in. If one contributor is tagging items as "graduate students" and another contributor is tagging similar items with a write-in variation like "gradstudents", this kind of naming inconsistency can also make it more difficult for users to find content. The best tagging policy will vary by the needs of your organization, but we believe a good initial policy should offer twenty to thirty tags as default options in the Categorization tab, and limit contributors to three to five tags for any one content item. Whatever tagging policy you choose, aim for consistency with your contributors.

Which kinds of tags should be added? (Admin users only)

Below are examples of tags which might be used for content items in a physics department folder:

*Lecture Series * Climate Change * Astrophysics * Research * Internship Opportunities * Spring Classes * Fall Classes * Solomon * Strudwick * Biophysics * Particle Physics * Research * News * Graduate Students * Undergraduate * FAQ * Faculty Spotlight*

As you can see, not all of these tags are directly related to the physics department. Some are for subsets within the physics department like "Particle Physics," and some of the more generic tags could be applied to entirely separate university departments. How should they be used? Let's take as an example, the fact that there are various internship opportunities scattered throughout the university site. Each of those opportunities could be tagged as "Internship Opportunities", and then could be tagged by their relevant department. Those that are astrophysics-related, for example, could also be tagged "Astrophysics." In this way, anyone searching for astrophysics internship opportunities on the site would find the appropriately tagged item, even if the item was not located in a physics department folder. Alternatively, if the internship opportunities were grouped into the same folder, you could work around tagging each opportunity one at a time. A content rule could be created which causes certain tagged items to move to a certain folder after publication, which would identify them as internship opportunities. By using content rules and folders this way, individual tagging can be unnecessary.

To extend the example, let's take Solomon and Strudwick, who are two professors at this university. Would the names of each professor make a good tag? Possibly, but tags might not be the only way to find content by a specific professor. Sometimes the byline will link to the user's other content, and sometimes you could add a collection that lists the research folder URL for each professor.

Because tags are usually visible to all contributors and editors on a site, if a site uses too many tags, it might be hard to decide on the best tag. Remember that a folder's URL can indicate to the visitor what kind of content it contains, and this may be a better approach than tagging everything individually. Here are some general guidelines for creating tags:

1. Tags should not duplicate the folder organization. There is no need to have an additional tag for Physics or English if these items are already found in the Physics or English department folders.

2. Because tags are viewable by all content creators, they should not be specific to a certain folder.

3. Tags should be created with an idea of collections that will be later used to organize them. For example, you could make a useful collection called Internships for Departments which would contain links to pages in all departments which are tagged with the word "Internships." Tags for "FAQ", "Lecture Series" and "News" could be used to generate separate collections.

4. Tags are best used to make it easy to find content which would not easily findable by other means.

5. For smaller or specialized Plone sites, it might make more sense to use subject-related tags. If a Plone site were about the American Physics Society, it might make perfect sense to use tags for climate change, astrophysics and physics.

Limit the number of tags which are created

This might be more of a personal preference than a hard and fast rule, but since the interface for selecting tags is a drop-down list, you need to hold down the Control key in order to select multiple tags. This interface can become unwieldy if the list contains more than 20 choices. One way to manage this is to start with 15 or 20 tags and be very selective about whether additional tags can be added to the list. This is certainly a top-down approach to tags, and for some sites this may not be recommended.

An alternate approach might be to allow as many tags as possible into the list of possible tags and let users figure out which tags are the most useful. This approach has value because it reduces the need for the Admin user to predict which tags will be used most often.

Pre-populate your site with tags by creating a private dummy page

Content creators do not always have the right to create their own tags, and this can introduce a chicken-and-the-egg problem when the time comes to actually create tags. How does the Admin user know which tags to add before content is actually added?

I recommend that the content manager and Admin user prepare a list of possible tags to use before content is actually added. Periodically, this list will need to be revisited over time to determine if additional tags need to be added.

In contrast to the "folksonomy" approach of letting users tags their own content, the default Plone approach is much more restrictive. This can be a blessing in disguise though, because it forces content creators to limit their choices to those available. It also reduces the confusion caused by multiple tags with similar meanings, or with close variations in naming.

Periodically add more tags to the site for content creators

An out-of-the-box Plone site allows only users with the Manager role (i.e., Administrator) or Reviewer role to add tags for site content, but this limitation can be lifted, and the responsibilities could be delegated to a certain class of users. Also, some add-ons let Plone users add tags to content, and can allow you to set up a feedback mechanism whereby day-to-day content creators could suggest tags for a Plone administrator to add later.

Exclude certain items from appearing in navigation or searches

If an automatically generated collection or portlet contains too many items, it can make it much harder to find desired content. Besides modifying the collection itself, there are two additional ways to hide items from search results:

- **Exclude the item type to be excluded from search results**. On the Settings tab for individual items, there is an option to *Exclude from Navigation*.

- **Set an item type to be excluded from search results**. To do this, the Admin user goes to *Site Setup --> Search --> Search Settings*. There you can remove certain content types from search results. The Admin user can also do this by going to Site Setup --> Types and choose the content type in the drop-down menu and uncheck the *Visible in Searches* option for that content type.

Depending on your site workflow, you may have a way to make certain items visible to other logged in users, but not anonymous users.

Become familiar with all the different displays for content

The chapter on folders and collections discussed displaying and sorting content items in a folder. It is important to be familiar with each type of display so you can choose the ones with the most relevant and usable views. Also keep in mind that it is easy to arrange the order of items in a folder, so it can be useful to move manually a more important content item higher in the folder display than a less important item.

Resist the tendency to use default displays for all your folders

Plone includes several display options for folders while giving the owner the option to use a default content item at the root of a folder.

Some of the default displays are workable, but remember that they are simply containers. Visitors want to view actual content, not the containers for them.

- Department pages are perfect places to use a content item as the default display instead of a list view. In the physics department example, it would not be helpful to see a list of items in the folder (because there could be so many kinds of content inside). Folders which contain subfolders are generally not good candidates for default displays. Instead, you should create a page and use this page as the default view for the folder.

- If a folder contains items which are mostly uniform or contains nothing but subfolders, then choosing one of the default displays would be appropriate.

A folder which has a content item set as default view needs a way for its contents to be visible

Setting the default folder display to show a content item will prevent the visitor from seeing a messy folder view. The downside is that without this folder view, visitors have no way to know what items are contained inside it. That might very well be your intent, but it implies one of two things. First, you will need to update the default content item manually every time an item inside the folder has been published. (If the folder does not contain a lot of content or is not frequently updated, this is actually not as burdensome as it sounds). Second, you might arrange for a navigation portlet to appear whenever the visitor is viewing an item inside that folder. This portlet could contain other content items from that folder and provide an easy way to "jump sideways" to other places inside the same folder. (See the section called the section called "Navigation Portlets" [166].

Rearrange items in a folder so that the more important items appear on top

Contrary to what you might think, the order in which items appear in folder views is not automatic. You can manually select the order by going to Contents view and grabbing individual rows and moving them up and down. This can allow more important items to appear more prominently.

Use portlets to call attention to special pages and collections

Portlets are especially useful for context-specific information. Therefore, if you are inside the physics department folder, it is likely that you will be interested in physics-related news or announcements. Perhaps there are four or five reference pages which all Physics majors use; making them accessible anywhere from the physics department folders can be a good thing.

Static Text portlets don't sound as sexy as collection portlets or navigation portlets, but often they get the job done. Don't hesitate to use them.

Turn off unnecessary portlets

As we covered earlier, turning off portlets for certain folders can be a good thing. Portlets can be distracting, and they can take up much-needed space. If you turn off portlets off on one or both sides, you widen the viewing area for the content to be displayed. This can be ideal on personal pages, for example. Also, turning off portlets for certain folders prevents the site as a whole from having a "cookie-cutter feel."

Because portlets display underneath all the folders from which they were added, it might not be relevant when inside a nested folder. For example, it might make sense to have sports announcements appear as a portlet near the root of your site (and inside the folder marked Student Activities). On the other hand, why would you need the portlet for sports announcements to appear if you are looking at a physics folder or a faculty member's home page? See the section called "Hiding Portlets" [153]for how to turn off portlets.

Try to ensure uniformity in folders at the same level by using templates

In the university example, you would expect the landing page for all academic departments to look basically alike. On the other hand, you would also expect the pages for student activities to look distinct from the President's Office page, Alumni Affairs Financial Aid, and other specific pages.

One way to ensure uniformity is to make certain templates available to your content creators. For example, you could create a private folder called "Department Templates" which contains other useful templates applicable for most academic departments. The Admin user could copy this Template folder into the Academic Departments folder, rename the Templates Folder to the specific department name and then delegate full rights to someone in that department.

Because the templates are in a private state, they would not be visible to the public unless someone with reviewer rights first took the step of publishing them.

Use anchors and table of contents for long pages

One built-in feature for the page content type is the ability to create a list of table of content links if a page has multiple headings and subheadings. For more information, see the section called "Autogenerating a hyperlinked Table of Contents at the top of the page" [66].

Use the Move feature of Plone to reorganize the site

Plone allows you to reorganize content fairly easily on the site with its Move/Copy feature. Take advantage of it!

Planning any content site can sometimes be difficult, because it is often difficult to predict which folders will be populated with the greatest number of items. In the best examples of information design, an organization emerges from the content rather than trying to being pre-planned from the start. It is common to discover that some folders are storing more content than others. As long as the site's content creators have used internal links inside pages, it is relatively painless to move content into different sections of the site.

Enable the Review List portlet

This is more of a production tip than a usability tip. But if you have a reviewer role, there is a portlet specifically to let you see items waiting to be reviewed. Having easy access to the review list might ensure that you keep on top of your queue more assiduously.

Find a way to make popular items more prominent

Some items are going to receive more user hits than others, and your web metrics will indicate the breakdown of hits.

Remember that if certain items receive more hits than others, there is probably a reason. As we discussed earlier, inconsistency in tagging or tag naming can affect the accessiblity of your content items. Make sure popular items are not just popular simply because they were easier to find versus other items.

It is not a bad idea to create a special portlet for the most interesting items on the site. One possibility is creating a special tag like "Cool" or "Featured article" which can be displayed globally as a collection portlet.

Use collections for landing pages

Collections allow you to insert boilerplate text on the page with search results. This is an ideal feature for department pages since you can list contact information and other unchanging information on the top and let the rest of the URL contain a collection of links specific to that department.

Use collections judicially

Collections are wonderful. They are one of the best things about Plone because they allow users to construct very specialized queries and display them in a variety of ways. On the other hand, collections are not final destinations, and visitors are still more likely to want to read pages. For that reason, you should make an effort not to have two or more collections containing the exact same links. Having too much overlap on collections can frustrate users by making them unable to find new or different content.

Sure, some degree of link redundancy is acceptable, and can even benefiit your site to an extent. But if you see the same link listed on several places, that could discourage visitors from browsing.

Make RSS feeds from your site easy to find

Previous versions of Plone had a link called *RSS* which appeared somewhere on the page. In Plone 4, this feature has been turned off even though the RSS is still being created. But it still a good practice to manually create a page listing the most important RSS feeds and making this page accessible from anywhere on the site (by including a link to it on the footer for example). See also the section called "Making and Customizing Web Feeds " [195].

Using Search

Despite all this talk about navigation and usability, it's easy to overlook the usefulness of the search box for users to find the content they seek.

First, there is an option **Only in current section**. Checking this is especially useful if your site has lots of content or if you are unsure of what exactly you are looking for.

Figure 11.1. Plone Search Box

Checking "Only in current section" provides a useful way of excluding content from unrelated parts of the web site.

Secondly, and most importantly, when you start typing words into the search box, a drop-down box will show (almost instantaneously) the relevant content items. This is called **Live Search**. In a gigantic site, this feature may not be that useful, but for most sites, the real-time display of possible results definitely drives visitors to use your site's Search. This is far easier for a visitor than understanding the site's navigation structure. In Live Search it is not necessary to type whole words for it to start listing potential results.

Third, Live Search lets you exclude terms from results. For example, if you type **Africa -South** (with or without quotation marks) it will show items containing the word "Africa" but not items containing South Africa.

Perhaps we should differentiate between searching and browsing. You search when you already have a good idea about what you are looking for. You browse when you don't know what you are seeking or just want to discover the kinds of content which are available about a certain topic. On the other hand, the quick responsiveness of Live Search makes it easy to preview lots of content just by typing a few letters.

Figure 11.2. Live Search

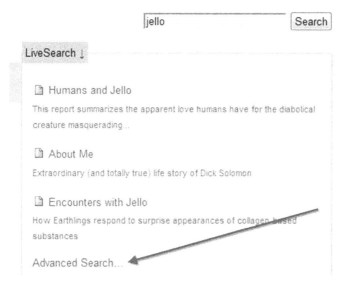

Clicking the Advanced Search link will let you do more exact searches.

Advanced Search

Although it may be easy to overlook, Plone actually has a powerful *Advanced Search* feature. A link to the *Advanced Search* page will be visible on the search results page after you try a simple search.

> *Advanced Search* only searches for complete words, so if your article contains the word **African** and you just type **Africa**, Advanced Search will not find it. By adding an asterisk, and typing **Africa*** instead, you will produce results containing the word "Africa" or "African." Typing in **"Africa or African"** (with the quotes) will bring results containing either word.
>
> Ironically, typing *Africa* in simple search might actually turn up a list of articles containing the word "African" because it displays results "live" and doesn't require that you type a complete word for you to see it in search results.

The *Advanced Search* page lets you filter the search results by various criteria. It also lets you sort existing search results.

On the left side of the web page is a link, *Filter the Results* which, when clicked, will reveal additional options. From here, you can include or exclude various content types from your search. You can also filter the results by how recently the item was published: yesterday, last week, last month, and ever.

On the right side of the *Advanced Search* page are three different ways to sort the search results:

- **Sort By Relevance**. Relevance is based on term frequency across all fields of an item. If the word "Africa" appears in 5 different places of a content item, for example, it will rank higher than another item where it appears only once.

- **Sort by Date** This will sort your items with the newest published items first.

- **Alphabetically**. This will sort your items in alphabetical order.

In previous versions of Plone, *Advanced Search* also let you search by user and review status, but this capability was recently removed. An Admin user, however, can still create collections which accomplish the same thing.

Chapter 12. Comments & Feeds

This chapter covers two important features which at some point Admin users will need to configure: comments and RSS feeds. Plone recently made improvements to how to configure these things.

Configuring Comments

Having web comments is a good way to engage visitors and add value to a website. Although third-party commenting systems like Disqus and Facebook are being used more frequently, managing comments through your CMS is still practical and offers certain advantages over just "farming it out" to a third-party. While these third-party services have their advantages (and some enterprising Plone developer is undoubtedly trying to integrate these services with Plone), Plone's built in commenting system should work well for most needs, and has the virtue of simplicity.

The two biggest challenges of comments are preventing spam and moderating user comments. I have run a WordPress blog for almost a decade, and the amount of inscrutable comment spam I have received to date must number in the millions. It's true that WordPress (and other platforms) use a distributed spam prevention service to reduce spam, but in Plone the comment moderation system is decent enough to prevent most spam attacks. This is partly because Plone uses a tighter security model than PHP-based systems, but also because it offers would-be hackers a smaller target than other CMS software. Furthermore, since Plone is deployed more often for organizational sites than for sites dedicated to group discussions, commenting is not as central a feature.

So overall, Plone sites receive a lot fewer spam comments, but on the other hand, Plone's comment moderation has fewer bells and whistles. Plone has a separate comment moderation menu (with the ability to do bulk approvals), but only Admin users will be able to access it. Ordinary users who are granted the right to approve comments (with the Reviewer role) must navigate to the content item's URL first to be able to view and approve comments. This can be unwieldy, but later on we will cover a workaround which notifies users with the reviewer role about new pending comments.

Enabling Comments

There are actually three different places where you could enable comments on your site:

- (*Manager Role Only*) Site Setup --> Discussion --> Globally enable comments. Mandatory if you want **any** commenting to be possible for any content type.

- *(Admin Role)* Site Setup --> Types --> (Dropdown option for content type) --> Allow Comments. **Note:** you are setting global defaults for *all* instances of this content type, so do not enable this unless you are sure it is what you want.

- *(Any Content Creator)* (Any Content Item) --> Edit --> Settings --> Allow comments. Here you can override global defaults about whether to show comments on a single item.

You must choose the **Globally enable comments** in Discussion before you can configure anything else. This doesn't mean that you are requiring all content to allow comments. It just means that the content creator will have the option to allow or deny them for an individual item.

> **Remember:** The content creator will *always* have the ability to enable or disable commenting by clicking the Edit --> Settings tab on a content item and checking/unchecking the Allow Comments box.

The most common way Plone is configured is to globally enable comments, but you can change the default behavior for content types to disallow comments. By doing this, you are leaving it at the content creator's discretion to enable comments. Having that extra manual step can be a pain, but it is probably the ideal arrangement for an organizational site and in keeping with Plone's emphasis on security.

This book only covers built-in content types for Plone. But it is easy for site developers to create custom content types whose default behavior is to allow comments. Suppose the site developers create a content type called "Blog Post" where comments are always turned on. That saves content creators the trouble of having to manually enable comments on each new item.

Configuring Requirements for Commenters

Now that an item can be configured to allow comments, how do you set restrictions or requirements for commenters?

To configure these kinds of things, you must be a user with the Manager role. This allows you to access the **Discussion** menu in *Site Setup*. This discussion control panel contains a variety of options which are self-explanatory.

1. *Should you require commenters to be a logged in user?* This is safer, but the Admin user needs to make sure that visitors can self-register. (Self-

registration is turned **off** by default. An Admin user can turn this on by going to Site Setup --> Security and checking the **Enable self-registration** box).

2. *Should you require that anonymous commenters provide an email?* Unfortunately when you do this in an out-of-the-box Plone site, the email will not be saved anywhere useful. It is not even used for an anonymous commenter to be notified about new comments. Perhaps a developer might configure something to do with this extra information, but for default Plone, it doesn't seem to matter.

3. *Should you require anonymous commenters to correctly answer a Captcha code?* There is an option to require a Captcha code, but this action will not become active until a user with the Manager role has installed the required third-party plugins.

4. *Should you enable user email notification for future comments?* If you enable this, only users who are registered with the site will be notified about future comments on this item. Anonymous commenters won't have this option – even if they provided an email.

Moderating Comments

While Plone now has the infrastructure and workflow to moderate comments, you still need to decide whether you want to moderate comments at all.

It may not be necessary to have moderation at all if only registered users are allowed to make comments, especially if only a few users are registered. In this case, moderation may need to be done infrequently. When comments go immediately into the moderation queue to await a reviewer's approval, it can potentially hinder a back and forth discussion because of the lag time in approving comments. This also creates extra work for moderators, and can be a problem especially if the person entrusted with moderating comments has other tasks and responsibilities.

Usually though, comment moderation is considered necessary – especially for comments from anonymous visitors.

To enable moderation of comments, a user with the Manager role must go to *Site Setup --> Discussion* and check the box, **Enable moderation of comments**.

Only users with the **Reviewer** or **Admin** role can moderate comments.

Once enabled, we are left with two questions: where does a moderator go to moderate comments? How does a reviewer know that comments are waiting in the queue?

The Moderator Queue. The Admin user will have a special option to access the *Moderate Comments* menu to view pending comments. To see it, the Admin should click on his or her user name on the top right of the screen and click **Moderate Comments** on the drop-down menu. After clicking on this, the Admin user will see a list of all pending comments and have the option of reading them and of approving/rejecting them in bulk.

Notification on the Content Item Itself. If you have the Reviewer role or Admin role, you can see pending comments when you visit the content item that received the comment.

Robert Nagle says:
Jul 18, 2013 10:51 AM

This is a test   Delete   Approve

Reply

——Add comment ————————————————————————

You can add a comment by filling out the form below. Plain text formatting. Web and email addresses are transformed into clickable links. Comments are moderated.

Comment ▪

Comment

Pending comments will appear in orange font on the URL of the published content item – immediately above the comment form.

The problem here is that users with the Reviewer role don't have a separate control panel for viewing all pending comments. So how would a user with only the Reviewer role know that there are pending comments awaiting action?

There are three ways to configure Plone to notify Reviewers and Admins about pending comments:

1. *(Manager Role Only)*. Plone Site Setup --> Discussion --> **Enable moderator email notification**. (If you want a particular user to be notified, you can also complete the field **Moderator Email Address**). This could easily become unwieldy if a site receives frequent comments.

2. **Add a Collection which lists all pending comments on one page**. This collection URL could be viewable only by users who have the right to approve comments. (See the section called "Collection Portlets" [163] and the section called "Collections" [94]).

3. Create a content rule to send an email to a user entrusted with the responsibility of moderating and approving comments. (See Chapter 9, *Using Content Rules* [142]).

The second method is an adequate solution which doesn't involve bombarding moderators with emails every time a new comment is made. Although this solution is fairly easy to configure, it involves a lot of steps, so let's go over them here. In this example, we are assuming that there is already a group called Comment-Reviewers whose members have reviewer rights for at least one folder. (This group can also have the global role of Reviewer, but this is not necessary). You have to be an Admin user to perform these steps.

1. Create a collection (anywhere you want). Call it something memorable ("Pending-Comments"). Make a note of its name.

2. Add these Search Terms: *Type is **Comment** and Review State is **Pending***.

3. Publish the collection.

4. Go to **Site Setup --> Users and Groups**.

5. Select the Groups tab and click on the **Comment-Reviewers** group you created earlier.

6. Log on as a member of the group **Comment-Reviewers**. Verify that the collection portlet appears.

The third solution (*Creating a content rule*) is something I wouldn't necessarily recommend, but I am mentioning purely for thoroughness. You can create a content rule which will email one or more reviewers whenever another comment is submitted. This isn't much different from the option in the Discussion control panel, but it's always an option.

Setting Options for how comments appear

The discussion menu (visible to users with Manager role in Site Setup), lets you set how input text is handled.

Under the option for *Comment text transform*, you have these options.

- *Plain Text*

- *HTML*. Users will be required to add html code for links, paragraphs, etc.

- *Markdown*. Users can use a special easy-to-learn formatting system which Plone can convert to HTML.

- *Intelligent Text*. Converts plain text into HTML where line breaks and indentation is preserved, and web and email addresses are made into clickable links.

Generally, the *Intelligent Text* option seems the most flexible and user-friendly.

If you are thinking of allowing anonymous comments, one thing you may to think about is that Plone 4.3 does not use the "rel=no-follow" attribute for comments. A few years ago, comment spammers were taking advantage of Google by inserting lots of links in spam comments in order to improve their search rankings. As a response, Google worked with several blogging and CMS platforms to include this no-follow code around user comments to tell search engines to ignore these links when computing prominence and authority in search results.

Because Plone doesn't use the no-follow tag, it will give "google juice" to any sites linked in comments. Some have argued that this isn't entirely a bad thing, but if your website is susceptible to lots of spammy comments, then your site might unwittingly be helping these spammers in their effort to game results on search engines.

There are two solutions to this problem: 1) Change the *Comment text transform* to plain text or 2) Require all commenters register on the site. The first option solves the problem, but at the cost of user convenience. The second option is generally reliable – although it would make it theoretically possible to use a "bot" to register users automatically. If you run a small, well-maintained site, and don't receive many comments, and those that are received are moderated intelligently, then it's probably not a big deal if a small handful of commenters are linking gratuitously to sites of dubious value. In this case, you should go ahead and choose Intelligent Text or HTML for your comment format. But if your site is receiving huge amounts of traffic, or if moderating comments has become time-consuming or if your website is receiving comments that are potentially dangerous or embarrassing, you may consider either solution, or a combination of the two to address it.

Making and Customizing Web Feeds

An RSS feed (short for Really Simple Syndication) is a family of web feed formats used when publishing frequently updated works (i.e., for blogs, news headlines, podcasts). An RSS feed includes the full or summarized text as well as metadata such as publishing date and authorship. It can also include images and multimedia as well as metadata (author, date, etc). These can be read by specialized RSS readers or aggregated from different places. More commonly, RSS feeds are used for mobile apps like Feedly and Flipboard. RSS feeds can also serve as notification systems for IT staff and media companies. If you google around for "feed notifier" or "RSS reader," you can find some good utilities which will notify you when something has been added to an RSS feed. Also, email clients like MS Outlook, Windows Live and Thunderbird generally let you keep track of RSS updates.

RSS feed is a generic name for several different kinds of syndication standards. Plone can generate feeds for the following RSS standards:

- RSS 1.0

- RSS 2.0

- Atom

- iTunes

Which standard is best or most compatible with the greatest number of RSS readers? From a purely technical standpoint, Atom seems to be the preferred standard. However, the difference between the standards is diminishing to the point that they are practically interchangeable. Most RSS readers are capable of reading any of these web feeds, and so it is not particularly vital to publish the same content in multiple RSS formats. Some websites do this anyway, especially for feeds detectable at the home page.

Media companies and content producers have had a long-standing debate on whether publishing RSS feeds reduces the overall amount of site traffic. If people can read your site via an RSS reader, for example, why would they ever become a member of your site's community? This may be a narrow view. In many cases, having RSS feeds does not erode overall web traffic and may in fact help drive traffic to the site. A lot depends on the audience's demographics as well as the device or application which people are using to read your content. Looking at my own behavior, I typically read articles via an RSS reading app on my iPad while riding the bus to and from work every day. In this case, I'm reading articles that I would not otherwise have time to get around to. Sometimes reading an article on my RSS reader causes me to check the website more often, and sometimes I never actually visit a website I have listed in my RSS reader.

Full Feeds or Partial Feeds? Another question is whether the RSS feed should contain the entirety of the content item or only an excerpt or summary of the content item. (To use the language of Plone, the question is to "render the body" of the content item or just include its "description"). Obviously providing a full feed benefits people who rely on RSS readers, but it also makes it easier for "scraper sites" (or spam websites) to swipe your content and to stick it around ads or use it to manipulate search engine rankings. A number of media sites provide only partial feeds to prevent precisely this occurrence. Providing a partial feed notifies people about new content while also forcing them to visit the actual site. On the other hand, when I'm on the bus catching up on RSS feeds on my iPad, having a partial feed is of little value when I don't have the ability to go online and read the entire article while travelling.

Another issue to consider is site performance. Providing too many full RSS feeds can end up slowing the web server's overall performance.

Since this book's first edition, Plone has improved its RSS support. Plone can generate more kinds of custom RSS feeds for use by human visitors and third-party software.

What is RSS in Plone?

Plone can create several different kinds of RSS feeds:

- **RSS feeds for folders**. Every time another item is published in a folder, it will be added to that folder's feed.

- **RSS feeds for collections**. This feed will show all the results of a collection, sorted in the way you specify. If a new content item is found to satisfy the collection's search terms, it will be added to the collection.

- **RSS feeds for individual search results**. (This must be enabled).

- **RSS feeds for the News folder**. (only the "News" content type).

- **RSS Feeds for Events**. (only the "Events" content type).

These are all possibilities. In fact, you can configure a Plone site so that only a small number of folders generate RSS feeds.

Typically you would expect to find one or more RSS feeds on the home page. In fact, there is a way in *Site Setup* to make an RSS feed detectable on the home page even though the feed itself may only be for a subfolder found deep within the site.

RSS feeds can have varying numbers of items in them. The default number that Plone sets is 15, but this can be changed. For certain situations it may appropriate to have 100 or more items in an RSS feed, and the number of items will depend mainly on your web server's overall performance, as well as your willingness to "retire" certain content items into the archive. Keeping the equivalent of about a month's worth of items in an RSS feed seems like a sensible initital strategy.

A Plone RSS feed will only display published content. Even if you are a logged in user with viewing rights, you will still not be able to see a private or pending content item in an RSS feed.

How do you know if a Plone site is generating RSS feeds?

When one or more RSS feeds are available on a URL, there should be an icon (usually orange) on the web page itself, so often it's just a matter of looking around the web page for it.

If this icon isn't there, however, it doesn't mean that the RSS feed is missing. In fact, Plone (and other CMS software) can be configured to generate RSS feeds but not display the feed icon.

Luckily, browsers usually have a built-in way of detecting whether the URL is associated with any feeds.

Firefox has 2 methods for detecting RSS methods. Either one works. The second method puts a shortcut on your toolbar for easy permanent access.

- Right click anywhere on the web page and choose **Page Info** and then the **Feeds** tab. It will show all available RSS feeds (and sometimes more than one!)

- Go to **View** --> **Toolbars** --> **Customize** and then choose the icon for Subscribe/Feeds and drag it to your Firefox toolbar. Remember that this assumes that the menu toolbar is already visible. If it is not visible, right-click on the top of the browser and make sure that **Menu Bar** is checked.)

Internet Explorer (IE) Tools --> **Feed Discovery** -->(see if a feed exists). If it does, IE will display it and give you some queries and options for subscribing and filtering. (If you don't see the Tools toolbar, right-click on the top toolbar and make sure **Menu Bar** is checked).

Chrome. At the time of this writing, the best way to discover RSS feeds in Chrome is to install an extension called **RSS Subscription Extension**. After installing it, you will see an orange feed icon on the URL bar. Pressing it will reveal more information about the RSS feeds on that particular URL.

Safari. The URL toolbar at the top will display a small blue rectangle with the letters RSS whenever a RSS is detected at a URL. When you click on this button, the full feed will display within the browser, along with some tools for filtering.

As mentioned above, Plone can be configured to show an inconspicuous RSS Feed link at the bottom of a content item. Once you click on the RSS feed option in the browser, the browser will show a "pretty" view of the RSS feed in the browser. Oftentimes in this pretty view, there is a way to view the "raw version" of the RSS feed. In Chrome for instance, after you go to the "pretty" view of the RSS feed, you will see a link on the right side of the browser labeled simply "Feed." If you press this, Chrome will show you the complete feed as XML source code. (i.e., the raw code view).

Configuring RSS Feeds *(Manager only)*

There are two places to configure RSS feeds: in *Site Setup* and in the *Syndication* tab for folders.

Only a user with the Manager role will have the ability to view and configure **Syndication** options in *Site Setup*. This is where you can set global defaults which can be modified at the folder or collection level.

The first thing to do is to check **Allowed**. This merely turns the capability on while still requiring it to be manually turned on.

Enabled by Default. Typically you will leave this *off*. It is better to require users to turn it on for specific folders and collections rather than allow it to be turned automatically on in dozens (if not hundreds) of places.

Search RSS Enabled. First, a collection does a much better job of creating custom RSS feeds based on certain criteria, but ordinary members or anonymous visitors won't normally have the ability to configure these things. It generally is a good idea to keep this feature turned *on*.

Show Author Info. Author information includes both the full name on the user account and the email associated with this user account. Only Atom and iTunes.xml actually include author information when this is enabled. Your needs may vary, but I think it's better to turn this feature *off* because some users may not want the email associated with their account to be so easily accessible.

Maximum Items. This sets a default number for the maximum number of items in a feed. The default number here, 15, is reasonable, but any users with access to syndication settings for folders and collections can easily override this number when desired.

Allowed Feed Types Generally, this text field controls which feeds show up as options in the *Syndication* tab for users. For example, if you want everybody on your site to use only Atom feeds, you could simply delete the other rows. You could also use this field to rename the label for each field. (The words which appear in the label are to the right of the vertical bar). Unless you wish to mandate that all site feeds use Atom, you should generally leave the defaults as they were.

Site RSS This two panel interface lets you pick which RSS feeds will be detectable from the home page. If you don't specify it here, don't worry. It will still be detectable from the folder or collection itself.

By moving certain folders or collections to the right panel, you can make their RSS detectable from the home page.

Show Settings Button. Check this box so that folder owners can have a syndication tab on their toolbar, thus allowing them to configure the RSS for that one folder or collection. You can use this to override RSS global defaults. This is a good thing, so be sure to check this.

Show Feed Link. If you check this, then a link saying simply "RSS feed" will appear wherever it is enabled. Because site feed readers often can detect feeds automatically on a site, it's not absolutely necessary to include this icon (especially because it's somewhat distracting). On the other hand, causing an icon to automatically appear on URLs with feeds can save time and effort of readers trying to figure out if an RSS feed actually exists. From a usability point of view, some sites have created a page showing a list of every RSS feed found on a website. A link to this RSS page could be listed at the footer of every URL.

Configuring Feeds for Folders and Collections

One new feature of Plone is that ordinary users can now enable and configure RSS feeds for folders and collections for which they have editing rights. This makes it easy to set up a RSS feed for a folder which shows new content being added to it.

If a user has editing rights for a particular folder, he or she will see an additional tab on the edit toolbar: **Syndication**.

The *Syndication* tab shows global defaults for syndication which can be overridden by the user in this specific folder. This tab contains 4 additional options.

Enabled. By default, this option is unchecked. It must be checked for an RSS feed to be detectable.

Feed Types. This option merely lets you choose one or more types of RSS which will be generated. Ideally, the defaults set here should be fine (as long as the Admin user has set the appropriate global defaults). Strategies for which RSS to use were discussed earlier in this chapter.

Unfortunately, the interface for setting Feed Types can be somewhat confusing (especially when viewed in the IE 10 browser).

Figure 12.1. Selecting a Feed Format for a Folder (Syndication Tab)

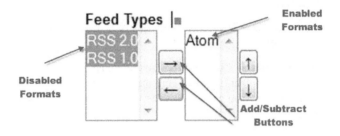

The forward arrow lets you enable a specific RSS format. The backward arrow lets you disable a specific RSS format.

Render Body. Checking this option will show the entire contents of an item. Earlier this chapter discussed the pros and cons of using full feeds vs. partial feeds. It's generally better to check this option, but you need to keep performance and security concerns in mind.

Maximum Items. The default number is shown, but you can easily increase or decrease this as needed. At some point though, a large enough number might reduce performance and even make the RSS less useful.

The RSS Portlet

RSS feeds are also used when configuring RSS portlets. (See the section called "RSS Portlets" [164]). The RSS portlet can show RSS feeds for external websites or internal RSS feeds. Keep in mind though, that if you are using a collection to create an RSS feed, you could use a collection portlet to achieve the exact same purpose.

Chapter 13. Site Setup

Site Administrator vs. Manager

For most of the book we have used the term "Admin user" to refer to a user with either the Site Administrator or Manager role. For many common operations, such as user management or creating content rules, both types of users are authorized to perform them.

The table at the top of this chapter summarizes the differences between the Manager role and Site Administrator role. Because of their more extensive access, both types of users have the capability to do major damage to a site. For this reason, make sure that users with one or both of these positions are technically proficient, careful and trustworthy. This chapter will provide an overview of most of the functions listed above, and also address functions available to the Site Administrator.

This chapter will cover the *Site Setup* control panel. If you are an Admin user, you can access Site Setup by clicking on your user name on the top right and selecting **Site Setup** under the drop-down options.

Aside from the **Users and Groups** menu on *Site Setup* (which you will need to use regularly to add and delete users), the Admin user will not typically need to make changes in Site Setup after initial configuration. More typically, the Admin user will go there to check which global settings have been set and gather enough information to verify if modifying a setting will solve a user problem. Sometimes, just enabling a feature in Site Setup is not enough, but it may still be necessary for a content owner or Admin user to enable it on a specific folder or page. Once enabled in Site Setup, a new tab will appear on the Edit toolbar. This is also true for Content Rules, Commenting and RSS feeds.

This chapter will provide a brief reference to some options relevant to content creation. Because this chapter is intended for content creators and routine Admin tasks, it will also provide a brief overview of features geared toward site developers.

Add Ons

An add-on is a set of features which are not enabled by default, but which can be turned on to provide additional special functionality. A user with the Manager role enables add-ons via the add-ons screen in *Site Setup*. It shows which add-ons are available to be added, and also lets you activate a specific add-on by clicking a check box. After you activate an add-on, a new configuration menu will often appear in *Site Setup*.

The default Plone installation comes with several add-ons which are disabled by default. The two disabled add-ons below are useful and relevant to content creators:

- **Workflow Policy Support.** This lets you customize a workflow for certain folders. See the section called "Changing Workflows for Individual Folders" [140].

- **Working Copy Support (Iterate)**. This allows one or more users to edit a temporary/private version of a content item which has already been published. See the section called "Checking Out Working Copies of Published Items" [107].

Here are some other important add-ons:

- **Diazo Theme Support**. Plone now supports a special kind of theme called Diazo. A Diazo theme typically consists of a static HTML page, JavaScript, CSS and a rules file (rules.xml). It dictates how content displays inside a web browser. A user with the manager role can upload a Diazo theme as a zip file. This user can also inspect and edit the theme directly inside the web browser.

- **HTTP Caching Support**. Plone provides a lot of things to tweak to improve site speed.

Both add-ons are more geared to the site developer and site planner and so are not discussed in detail here.

Calendar

There is a "calendar portlet" which will show a miniature calendar on the page, containing hyperlinks to events. This configuration screen lets you specify the workflow state of items that will appear on it as hyperlinks. For example, should private or pending items also appear on the calendar? You can configure that here.

Content Rules

See Chapter 9, *Using Content Rules* [142] for more information.

Discussion Settings

This menu lets you configure defaults for commenting and moderation. See the section called "Configuring Comments " [190] for more information.

Errors

The manager can view error logs through the Plone interface.

HTML Filtering

The TinyMCE editor will allow you to paste raw HTML code into the text field, but certain elements and attributes will be stripped out for security reasons, including tags like script, object, applet, embed, and style. The HTML filter settings allow the Admin user to specify which elements and attributes should be stripped out and which should not.

One common issue that arises when pasting content into TinyMCE editor is that it will also paste the HTML classes of the original web page you pasted from, and this information will not be filtered out. Most of the time, this does not cause any problems except for making the raw HTML code messy to view. In rare cases, the CSS classes of the inserted HTML code may conflict with the CSS classes of your organization's site. For example, perhaps you pasted text from another web page into TinyMCE and you notice that a lot of the paragraphs start with this: **<p class="article_main_text"**>. If you wanted Plone to strip out **class="article_main_text"** from every p element that you paste, you would need to add a filtered class.

To add a filtered CSS class so Plone will exclude it:

1. Go to **Site Setup** when logged on as the Admin user. Choose **HTML Filtering**.

2. Click the **Styles** tab. Click the **Add Filtered Class** button.

3. Type in the specific class name you wish to filter.

Figure 13.1. Filtering an HTML Class

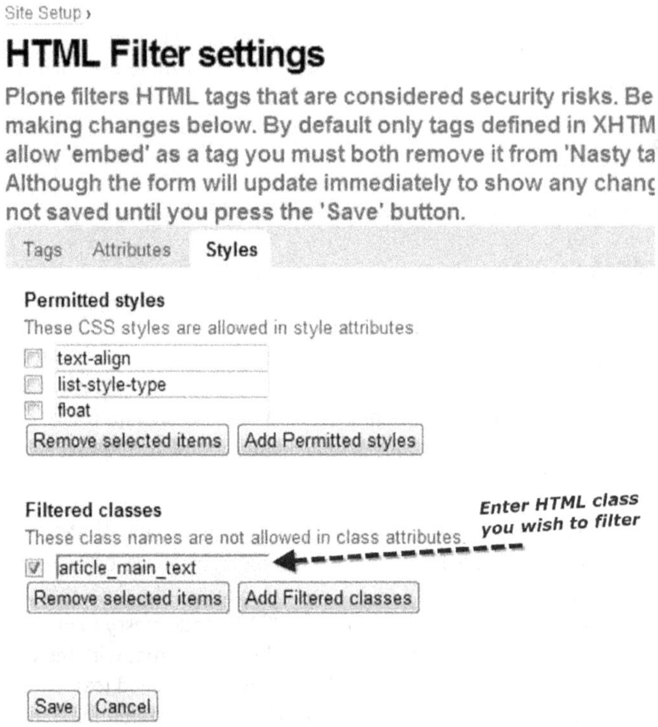

Site Setup ›

HTML Filter settings

Plone filters HTML tags that are considered security risks. Be
making changes below. By default only tags defined in XHTM
allow 'embed' as a tag you must both remove it from 'Nasty ta
Although the form will update immediately to show any chang
not saved until you press the 'Save' button.

Tags   Attributes   **Styles**

Permitted styles
These CSS styles are allowed in style attributes

☐ text-align
☐ list-style-type
☐ float

[Remove selected items] [Add Permitted styles]

Filtered classes   *Enter HTML class*
These class names are not allowed in class attributes *you wish to filter*

☑ article_main_text   ◄---------

[Remove selected items] [Add Filtered classes]

[Save] [Cancel]

You can explicitly filter out or permit an HTML class on the HTML filtering menu.

Explicitly permitting a style attribute. The process for adding a permitted style
is similar to adding a filtered class. The only difference is that you start by clicking
the **Add Permitted Styles button**. This might be useful if you pasted a great deal
of HTML which already had inline styling information which you'd like to enable.

Image Handling

When a contributor uploads an image, the manager can choose different size options to render the image in, but generally the defaults will be fine.

Markup

The Admin user can determine which kinds of markup the Plone text editor can
accept. A markup language is a system for annotating text with instructions about
presentation or processing. HTML is one example of a markup language (and

perhaps the most common kind). Here are some examples (and even more can be added).

text/html
text/plain
text/plain-pre
text/restructured
text/structured
text/x-python
text/x-rst
text/x-web-intelligent
text/x-web-markdown
text/x-web-textile

Having the ability to input markup languages is useful because it becomes easier to import specially formatted content from another source, like another content management system. Restructured text, for example, is used fairly frequently for Python applications. In general, though, most content creators should not need to worry about these alternative text formats except in special cases.

Important Note: For users to be able to choose one of these alternative formats for input, they will need to disable TinyMCE on User Preferences and instead select **None** as the preferred content editor.

Enabling Wiki Markup

Plone has some generic wiki functionality, but before you can make use of it, it must be enabled in the Control Panel under *Markup --> Wiki Behavior*.

Once this is checked, a user can use double parentheses in Plone's editor to create a "wiki link" (i.e., a hyperlinked topic which becomes a new page whenever someone clicks on it to edit it).

Navigation

The first two options below are related to folders which appear at the site root. The remainder of the settings only affect what kinds of content items appear in the navigation portlet. For more information, see the section called "Navigation Portlets" [166].

- **Displayed content types**. The content types that should be shown in the navigation portlet and site map. By unchecking any content item, you can prevent it from being findable.

- **Filter on workflow state**. Here you can control whether items which have not been published will appear in the navigation portlet and sitemap. If this option is <u>unchecked,</u> then there will be no filters and items in *all* states will be shown in the navigation portlet and sitemap. If this option is <u>checked,</u> then only the items which are checked will appear in the navigation portlet and sitemap.

  The checkboxes below this option list various workflow states. Generally a safe configuration to pick is to check *Filter on workflow state* and then check <u>only</u> the checkbox for *Published* state.

- **Show items normally excluded from navigation if viewing their children**. Again, this refers solely to the navigation portlet. This option is used only under special situations. For example, if you excluded private folders from navigation portlets, but happen to be on a published page which is inside this private folder, checking this would display the private parent folder in the navigation portlet. This feature is used rarely.

Search Settings

Here are some of the features of search settings.

- **Enable Live Search**. This is turned on by default and control whether the Search box will display a live drop-down of predictive results as the user is typing.

- **Define the types to be shown in the site and searched**. In new installs, every content type is enabled by default, but it would be a good idea to consider turning off some types. For example, images will often not need to show up in search results and can add unnecessary noise. There are also good reasons to not make collections or links searchable. Files and comments should be acceptable to include because their title and description should indicate to the visitor whether it is relevant to the search.

Security

Here are some settings relevant to content creators:

1. **Enable self-registration**. Self-Registration should be enabled; otherwise, a user will not be able to login. This is disabled by default.

2. **Enable User Folders** Previous Plone versions let each user have a dedicated folder, but this was disabled for Plone 4. Using this option caused problems because the user would publish content in his own folder and then need to move the published content elsewhere. Content rules can

now be configured to automatically move an item to the desired location on the site after publication. However, many users find it easier just to add/edit an item in the same place where it will be published. Also, any folder owner can give another user full rights over a folder, and that essentially accomplishes the same thing.

3. **Allow anyone to view 'about' information**. Unchecking this will hide information about who created the content item and when it was last modified. This might help if your site is for a company and the individual's name is not important or relevant. Even when this option is unchecked, logged-in users will still be able to view user information and history/modification dates.

Site (Global Settings)

Below is a brief overview of global site settings:

- **Site Title:** This shows up in the title bar of browsers and in syndication feeds. The Admin user should definitely customize this to display the site's title.

- **Site Description**. The site description is available in syndicated content and search engines. Keep it brief.

- **Expose Dublin Core metadata**. This exposes the Dublin Core properties as metatags. Dublin Core is an international standard for metadata. How important it is to expose this metadata depends on whether you feel it would help on search results and whether content creators are actually completing these fields.

- **Expose sitemap.xml.gz**. This exposes your content as a file according to the sitemaps.org standard. You can submit this to compliant search engines like Google, Yahoo and Microsoft. This is generally recommended, since it allows these search engines to more intelligently crawl your site.

- **JavaScript for web statistics support**. This is for enabling web statistics support from external providers like Google Analytics. Paste the code snippets that are provided, and they will be included in the rendered HTML as it was entered near the end of the page.

Theming

If the site has enabled Diazo themes (an optional add-on which is included with every Plone install), a user with the Manager role will see another control panel here for themes. This control panel will let the user with the Manager role swap themes, inspect themes using a browser-based window, and make some configuration changes.

TinyMCE

You can configure general settings for the TinyMCE editor on *Site Setup* too.

Layout Tab

- **Enable resizing of the editor window.** This option gives you the ability to enable and disable resizing of the editor window. If the editor width is set to a percentage, only vertical resizing will be enabled.

- **Enable auto resizing of the editor window.** This option gives you the ability to enable and disable automatic resizing of the editor window depending on the content.

- **Editor width**. This option gives you the ability to specify the width of the editor in pixels or percentages.

- **Editor Height**. This option gives you the ability to specify the height of the editor in pixels. If automatic resizing is enabled, this value is used as the minimum height.

- **Writing Direction.** If this option is available, you can specifiy the default writing direction. You would use this for some languages like Hebrew or Arabic write from right to left instead of left to right.

- **Enable contextmenu.** This option gives you the ability to enable and disable the use of the context menu. You will see the context menu if you right-click when your mouse is inside the text-window. It will provide some Plone-specific options: Cut/Copy/Paste/Insert or Edit Image/Alignment/Insert New Table. However, the Cut/Copy/Paste usually doesn't work because the popular browsers don't allow cut/copy/pasting through a browser-based context menu. The browsers will warn you about this and suggest using a keystroke combination instead (Control C, Control X, Control V). In fact, all of the functions in this special context menu duplicate functions already found in the browser or on the TinyMCE toolbar, so you can safely disable this feature without problem. (In fact, users may incorrectly regard the warning message as a bug, not a feature).

- **Choose the CSS used in WYSIWYG Editor area.** This option enables you to specify a custom CSS file that extends the theme content CSS. This CSS file is the one used within the editor (the editable area). Note that this

CSS applies only to the editing environment, not to the final page when published.

- **Adding Styles to the Dropdown Style List.** The Styles text field lets the Admin user add custom styles to appear in the style pulldown. Format is **title|tag** or **title|tag|className**, one per line.

    - **red 10 pt Georgia|p|red-10pt** . Result: In the drop-down menu, the user would see one option as **red 10 pt Georgia**. If selected, the paragraph which was selected would be entirely in red color 10 point Georgia. The HTML code would be `<p class="red-10pt">This is the text </p>`

    - **superscript|span|super** Result: In the drop-down menu, the user would see one option listed as **superscript**. If selected, the passage selected will look this this: `<p> <span class="super-script">This is the text </span> and this is more text. </p>`

    Important Note: A user with the Manager role will still need to edit the actual CSS file (and include the name of the style along with a declaration in proper CSS syntax). How to do this is not covered here because different Plone sites have different methods for editing or accessing the CSS files.

- **Adding table styles to the drop-down Style List.** Adding table styles to the drop-down style list is similar to adding other custom styles. Keep in mind that you will need to add the name of your style here and include a CSS declaration in your Plone CSS file as well.

Additional TinyMCE Toolbar Buttons

TinyMCE comes with other toolbar buttons which can be enabled. Here is a list of toolbar buttons not normally turned on by default: *Save, Cut, Paste, Paste as Plain Text, Paste From Word, Undo, Redo, Find/Replace, Underline, Strikethrough, Subscript, Superscript, BackColor, ForeColor, Insert Custom Character, Insert/Edit Media, Insert Horizontal Ruler, Insert Advanced Horizontal Ruler, Insert Date, Insert Time, Emotions, Insert Page Break, Print, Preview, Spellchecker, Remove Formatting, Cleanup Messy Code, Toggle Guidelines/Invisible Objects, Visual Control Characters On/Off, Insert/Edit Attributes.*

The majority of these buttons may seem limited in function, and keep in mind that the same functionality can often be found through the user's browser. For example, you don't really need a spellcheck button in TinyMCE because modern browsers already have a built-in spellchecker (i.e., the red squiggly lines that magically appear under the word when you misspell it). Sometimes a button requires additional configuration for it to actually work. For example, the *Insert/Edit*

Media button can allow you to add URLs to videos, but the Admin user needs to set up appropriate HTML Filtering options on *Site Setup*.

Here are some general recommendations about how an Admin user can tweak the global TinyMCE settings to improve the user experience for content creators.

- **Increase toolbar width**. The default width of 440 pixels is too small, and increasing the width will let you put more buttons on the toolbar. Although putting too many buttons can make the toolbar look too "busy," extra buttons can really make the content creator's job easier. Ideally you should aim for a width where all the TinyMCE buttons can fit on two rows. I have found that increasing the width to **550 or 600** works very well.

- **Save Button**. Putting a Save button on the toolbar makes it easier for the content creator to save often, and also allows the user to stay in Edit mode after the Save button is pressed. By contrast, when a content creator presses the Submit button to save work, Plone brings this user to the View mode instead of Edit Mode. **Note:** The only limitation here is that saving the item by pressing the TinyMCE button does not save a new version for Plone's versioning feature. New versions are added only if you press the Save button at the bottom of the *Save* area.

- **Paste as Plain Text** and **Paste from Word**. These are great buttons new to TinyMCE. **Paste as Plain Text** helps when pasting stuff from a browser window or a PDF file. **Paste from Word** is a great option, because manually pasting content from Word typically outputs as very messy HTML Code with lots of Microsoft-specific styles on each line. This makes the code unwieldly to inspect or edit. **Paste from Word** will strip all these Microsoft styles and leave only basic styling.

- **Undo/Redo**. Although Control-Z is usually sufficient to undo your last action, having buttons for Undo and Redo make it that much easier to undo major editing mistakes.

- **Insert Custom Characters**. Expert users probably already know how to add special characters using their keyboard. For casual users, however, having this button provides a quick way of adding a symbol for a Euro, trademark, accent marks, em dashes and a whole lot more.

- **Forecolor**. This lets you set a custom color for some text. Although the site styles are usually sufficient, individual users may find it useful to use custom font colors in certain circumstances.

- **Insert Non-Breaking Space**. This can help for adding extra spaces or for filling a table cell with empty space until you have content to add to it.

Here are some other buttons which might be useful to specific kinds of users and sites.

- **Insert/Edit Anchors**. This new button lets you create linkable spots in the middle of an article. Instead of linking to the top of the page, an anchor allows you to link to a certain location in the page instead. While a tech savvy user could just add anchors in HTML mode, this button makes the process much more convenient.

- **Insert/Edit Attributes**. This pop-up dialog contains two fields for **Text Direction** and **Language**, and this could be useful for multilingual sites.

- **Subscript** and **Superscript**. This button is particularly useful if your site features academic reports, which require special font formatting for parenthetical citations, references, or addendums.

Types

The **Types** menu controls a lot of global options for content types.

Figure 13.2. Setting Global Defaults for the "Page" Content Type

Type Settings

Up to Site Setup
Workflow, visibility and versioning settings for your content types.

Click the dropdown menu to configure settings for a different content type

Defaults are set here for all instances of this content type (You can override some of these settings for individual items).

Typically these settings are not changed after the site is launched, and usually the default content types are left alone. In the rare cases when the manager tweaks the workflow after deployment, it is to make the approval process "less annoying," or conversely, "more strict."

Globally addable	If this option is not checked for the selected content type, you will only be able to add that content type where it is explicitly allowed.
Allow Comments	By default, this option is unchecked. Content creators will always be able to enable or disable comments on the Properties tab

	of the content item regardless of what is specified here. In *Site Setup --> Discussion*, there is an option, *(Globally enable comments)* which must be enabled before comments can even appear as an option.
Visible in Searches	You'll usually want to leave most content types visible in searches. Even though a type like Files can't be understood by Plone, files can still contain useful searchable metadata about the file, such as the author, tags, or a modification date.
Versioning Policy	Manual vs. Automatic vs. No Workflow. It's recommended to version most content types, except files (which are usually binary and can't be versioned anyway).
Manage Portlets assigned to this type	Content Type Portlets are special portlets which pop up on the left or right of the screen whenever the visitor is looking at that content type. Clicking on this link will allow the Admin user to create or edit a portlet that is specifically for this content type. For more about portlets, see the section called "Using the Portlet configuration screen" [157].
New Workflow	You can change the default workflow for a content item, and could either use one of the workflows that comes with Plone or create a customized one yourself.

Users and Groups

From here, you can create user accounts, add users to groups and configure roles. See Chapter 7, *Sharing* [111] for more.

Zope Management Interface

The Zope Management Interface (ZMI) lets a user with the Manager role view and edit global settings and run simple administrative tasks. You can also access the ZMI by typing **http://myhost.com/manage** where myhost.com is the web host. Generally, it is easier and safer to make changes in Plone rather than going to the ZMI. Here are some basic tasks which you can accomplish in the ZMI without having to do any coding.

- Undoing deletions by a user. (See the section called "Undoing Deleted Content " [124].)

- Setting a purge policy for how many revisions of an item to save. (See the section called "Advanced Topic: Limiting the version history" [109].)

- Giving a normal user or group member the right to manage portlets for a folder. (See the section called "Giving Group Members the rights to manage or add Portlets in certain folders " [126].)

- Adding/Editing the MailHost. From ZMI root, choose *MailHost (Mail server settings for outgoing mail)*.

- Personalizing the site's 404 error messages. From ZMI root, choose *portal_skins --> plone_templates --> default_error_message*. Click the **Customize** button and then in the Edit area, add a personalized error message in the appropriate spot. Then click the **Save Changes** button. Note: Be careful not to change the TALES code in this file. As long as you edit only the portions containing the boilerplate text for the error messages, you will be ok.

Glossary

Admin User	Phrase used in this book to refer to functions or capabilities which can be performed by users with either the Manager role or Site Administrator role. Outside of this book, this phrase doesn't mean anything specific to Plone.
Administrator	Somewhat ambiguous term which in Plone refers either to a user with the Manager role or the Site Administrator role. For this book, the term is used mainly in situations which would be true with either kind of user. In the Plone Users & Groups control panel only, it refers to a group that gives all users the Manager role.
Anchor	Way of referencing a specific part of a page rather than the page in general. If you want a hyperlink to link to a certain destination, you will include in the destination in the HTML code something like `<a name="testanchor1"></a>` . This code will be invisible to site visitors but allow other sites to link directly to the anchor rather than the page itself. The hyperlink referencing the anchor will look like this: `<a href="http://wwww.test.com/index.html#testanchor1">my link </a>` .) The Plone rich text editor not only lets you put anchors on the page; it also stores it as an internal link so that it is available as a possible link on the Insert/Edit Link dialog.
Breadcrumb	In the context of web design, this is a navigation aid which lets the user keep track of his place in a website. It usually includes the path of the current location in the navigation bar, with each component of the location separated by an icon or punctuation such as the "greater than" sign (>). Each part of the location is in fact a separate hyperlink which goes to a progressively higher parent web page. Plone by default includes these breadcrumbs. Nonetheless it is better to give users other ways to browse through content and not rely solely on the breadcrumbs (which can be cumbersome when dealing with a deep hierarchy of content items.
Collection	Generic Plone content type which contains other content types. Collections allow you to create a filtered list of content items using one or more criteria. These items

which appear in the collection may come from different folders or different users. Even though a collection is mainly a stored query of your site's content, in fact it has many similarities to other content items and especially folders. **Note:** Typically only users with the Site Administrator or Manager role will have the ability to create and edit collections.

Content Rules

Set of instructions devised by the Admin user from the Content Rules control panel. You can use a content rule to create triggers for user actions. You can apply content rules to specific folders.

Content type portlet

See Type of portlet which appears on a web page for a specific content type. Ex. A content type portlet might be configured to appear whenever Plone shows an Event content type. Unlike other portlets, the Plone Administrator configures content type portlets need with the portlet manager but on Plone Site Setup --> Types. However, they can be hidden from the portlet manager.

Dashboard

Configuration screen that appears at the top right when a user logs in. To access it, choose the drop-down options under your login name and select "dashboard." It contains the latest content created by a user as well as a reviewer portlet (and possibly other portlets).

Dublin Core

Set of metadata elements which describe and catalog the content on a web page. In Plone, many of the fields in the edit tabs (date, rights, language, etc.) correspond exactly to Dublin Core metadata standards. In fact, the site administrator can enable the Dublin Core properties to appear as metatags in the actual HTML code (**Plone Site Setup --> Site**).

External link

A full absolute URL that exists outside of your Plone site. Example: *http://www.google.com*

Folder

In Plone, a folder is a content item which can contain other content items. Folders can be used to make sections in the website. Unlike a directory on a computer or on an FTP site, they don't refer to specific files; instead they refer to objects that exist in the Zope object database. It would therefore be impossible to copy a Plone folder onto your hard drive. You can configure the view when a reader goes to the URL of a Plone folder. Although in many cases the reader will see a list of folder contents if the user visits the folder URL, you can set a page as the default view.

Group Portlet

Type of portlet which pops up to members of a certain group. Groups are configured in the **Site Setup** --> **Users and Groups** by the Admin user.

HTML filtering

Stripping certain HTML tags from text input that might be dangerous. Plone and other content management systems will typically remove or strip a number of tags to remove the possibility of someone typing or pasting a malicious script into the rich text editor. As a result, some paste actions may not appear to work in the rich text editor. The Admin user has the ability to modify what kind of HTML code will be filtered in the web editor.

Intelligent Text

Text format which converts plain text into HTML where line breaks and indentation is preserved, and web and email addresses are made into clickable links. This is one of the options for user comments.

Internal link

Reference to a URL within the same Plone site. Typically the user makes an internal link by using the TinyMCE interface by browsing through Plone content and selecting the item that the internal link should link to.

Live Search

Refers to the feature in the Plone search box which will show possible search results underneath the search box, in real time as the user is inputting the search term.

Link integrity

The tendency for URLs to remain valid over time. Plone includes a *link integrity checker* feature that will notify you when trying to delete content if another content item is linking to it. That will give the content creator the opportunity to take corrective action or to notify a creat or of the linking page. This link integrity checker is turned on by default but can be turned off from the Plone control panel by the Plone manager. (Go to **Site Setup** --> **Editing**). Note that there are third party applications or even web applications that can produce regular reports about invalid links (and the site administrator could run an analytics program to analyze the URLs that result in 404 error messages).

Manager (role)

Powerful Plone role which allows full access to and use of the Plone control panel, including the Zope Management Interface.

Locking

In content management, this refers to the ability of one user to edit a content item exclusively. Plone uses a system of "soft locks" which will notify you whenever you try to edit a content item at the same any user is trying to do so. However, users have the ability to "break the lock" on locked content. The locking feature is intended more as a "friendly notification system" rather than a way for one user to edit a content item exclusively. However, this is not a tragedy; even if one user were to step on another user's toes, Plone's versioning capability would make it relatively easy to reconstruct the series of edits which were made.

Object

An object is a generic word used to describe all content types which are put into the ZODB. In general objects do not exist on the file system. That means that content items which we are used to thinking as files on our computer (.jpg, .doc or .pdf files) actually reside in the ZODB itself instead of being located in a specific directory on the web server. These content items can be accessed from Plone (and indeed can be downloaded from Plone), but they are not saved as files except in the database itself.

Product

Another term for add on in Plone.

Plone

According to the Plone.org docs, the word "Plone" originally comes from the electronic band Plone that used to exist on the Warp record label. The music is playful and minimalistic. The founders of Plone-the-Software (Alan Runyan and Alexander Limi) were listening to Plone-the-Band when they met (as well as during the initial coding/design of Plone) – and one of the original quotes floating around at the time was '*Plone should look and feel like the band sounds.*'

Portlet

In Plone, a portlet is a web component which displays on the left or right of the primary page content. Although the function of a portlet varies, usually a portlet displays supplemental information or quick links to relevant URLs or user-specific information. For the anonymous visitor, a portlet will appear as a sidebar or box on the left or right of the screen.

Retract

Workflow action when a contributor or editor a moves an item from a Published state into a Private state. Depending on the workflow settings, items which are retracted can later resubmitted or republished.

Rich Text Editor

Web-based editor which is incorporated into a CMS. What distinguishes a rich-text editor from a simple text editor is: 1) the fact that in the editing panel "What You See is What You Get" (WYSIWYG) and 2) the interface includes buttons at the top that assign styles to parts of the content. The Admin user can usually set the default rich text editor (although users can potentially change the default option in the **Preferences** menu). Previous versions have used Kupu as the default rich text editor, but for Plone 4, TinyMCE is now the default.

RSS

Abbreviation for Really Simple Syndication. On the Internet, it refers to a family of web feed formats used when publishing frequently updated works (i.e, for blogs, news headlines, podcasts). An RSS feed includes the full or summarized text as well as metadata such as publishing date and authorship. These can be read by specialized readers such as Google Reader. Plone can be configured to generate RSS feeds, but an RSS portlet can also be configured to display the RSS feeds from third party sites.

SEO

Acronym for Search Engine Optimization, the study of tailoring your content for Google and other search engines.

Site Administrator

Powerful Plone role which allows access to and use of the the Plone control panel, but does *not* provide the ability to install add-ons, edit themes or control system cache.

Site Setup

Control panel web page in Plone. A link to Site Setup should appear at the top right side of the page if the logged in user possesses manager, site administrator or Zope administrator privileges. Typically the options that appear on this panel are specific to Plone. However, for

	users with the manager role, this control panel also includes a direct link to the ZMI.
Syndication	See *RSS* above.
Tags	A kind of keyword which a content creator can select or add to a content item. When on the **Edit** display, you can select or insert a tag by switching to the Categorization tab.
Theme	Group of template files which content items appear on a URL and the layout/presentation of these items. These files are uploaded onto the web site and are generally not editable by content creators or even visible to them. A theme may be created for a specific site, purchased by a third party or downloaded for free from Plone.org. Plone 4.3 include support for the Diazo theme engine; when "Diazo theme support" is enabled, a control panel will be visible to Site Administrators and Managers to inspect, edit, upload and swap themes.
TinyMCE	Open text WYSIWIG rich-text editor included by default with the Plone content management system. As a software project, it exists separate from Plone (and is used by other CMS's like Drupal and Wordpress.
Versioning	Plone feature which allows you to keep a record of different versions of the same content item. While logged in, you can access it by clicking the **History** link. Some reasonable definition here. Versioning includes the ability to compare two different versions of the same content item and also to revert to the prior version.
Webdav	(*Short for Web-based Distributed Authoring and Versioning*). Internet standard for managing files and web pages with a web server as though they were folders on your local machine. You can use a webdav client on your local machine to upload files directly to the Plone server. Plone has some webdav support; webdav clients are commonly used by Plone users to upload larger files (such as video) directly to a Plone server without needing FTP access.
Working copy	This allows a content creator to edit a page after it has already been published. Essentially it is a second "cloned" version of the published version of the page.

When it is being edited (and even saved), the published version will still be available. However, the published version will become a versioned archival copy after the working copy is checked in again. **Note:** this feature needs to be enabled by the Site Administrator.

Workflow
Process by which content is submitted, reviewed and approved for publication by more than one person. Plone allows administrators to set up a custom workflow while offering several workflows out of the box: simple workflow, one-step workflow, community workflow and intranet/ extranet workflow. Note that one Plone site could potentially use different workflows depending on the location of the item and the item type.

ZMI
The Zope Management Interface (ZMI) refers to the web interface which allows the user to make customizations to the ZODB, check permissions and run routine database operations. Generally, only a user with the Manager role can access the ZMI.
See Also Plone .

ZODB
Abbreviation for Zope Object Database which stores the content data. Learning about the ZODB is beyond the scope of this book; it is sufficient to know that (for the most part) content items are not stored on the file system on the web server but are stored within the ZODB itself. That means that if you upload an image or PDF into Plone, this image or PDF will not exist anywhere on the web server but will be stored in the ZODB itself. In some cases, the site developer or system administrator will install a separate product to handle media files or larger files by putting them in a certain directory on the server's file system itself. However, the out-of-the-box Plone does not include this functionality, and it must be separately installed and enabled.

Zope
Generic name of the application server running Plone. The Zope Management Interface (ZMI) refers to the web interface which Plone Administrators can use to make customizations to the ZODB, check permissions and run routine database operations. Generally, only a user with the Manager role can access the ZMI.

Appendix A. Basic Plone Workflows

Even though Plone provides tools for the Admin to customize workflows, Plone includes several workflows out of the box. They are suitable for many purposes.

Simple Workflow

Figure A.1. Simple Publication Workflow

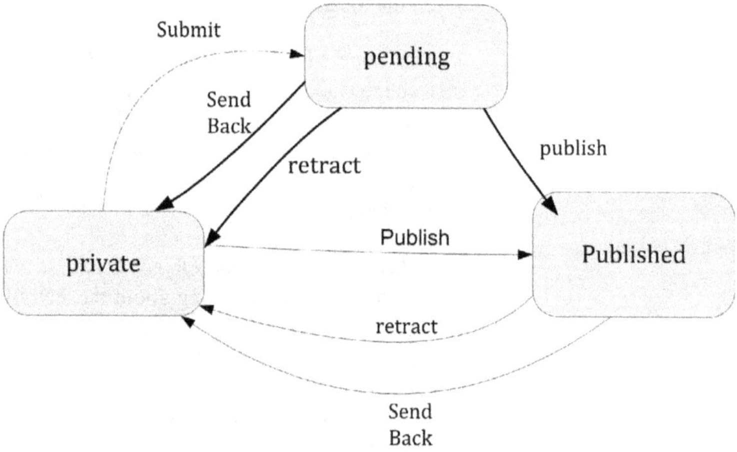

Plone's default workflow is referred to as the "Simple Workflow." Users who are not logged in can only access items subject to this workflow model which have been published.

The simple workflow includes three states:

Private
: (*red*) Beginning state newly added items are automatically given the "Private" state. A private item can only be viewed and edited by its owner or the Admin.

Pending Review
: (*orange*) An item in this state has been submitted for review so that an editor can either publish or retract it. Both owners and reviewers can view the item, but only reviewers can make changes to it while in this state.

Published
: (*blue*) Any visitor to the website can view published items. They will also be listed in portlets for anonymous viewers

to access. After being published, an item can be edited by its owner as well as any editor.

The state changes reflect the following actions:

Submit for Publication	Transition from the "Private" state into the "Pending review" state. The transition can be initiated by either the owner of the item, an editor, or the Admin.
Publish	Transition from the "Private" or "Pending review" states into the "Published" state. A reviewer or Admin changes the state of the item to "Published," thereby designating it as official content of the website.
Send Back	Transition from the "Pending review" or "Published" states back into the "private" state. A reviewer thus rejects an item for publication on the website. The author can then resubmit the item for further review after having reworked it.
Retract	Transition from the "Pending review" or "Published" states into the "Private" state. The owner pulls an item out of the published state in order to rework it and resubmit it for publication at a later time, for example.

One State Workflow

In this workflow model, items are automatically given the "Published" state. This is the only state available, and there are no state changes. If an item subject to this workflow model should no longer be visible, it needs to be deleted from the website.

Community Workflow

Items in the community workflow are visible to all visitors to the website, as long as those items have not explicitly been issued the "Private" state.

Figure A.2. Community Workflow

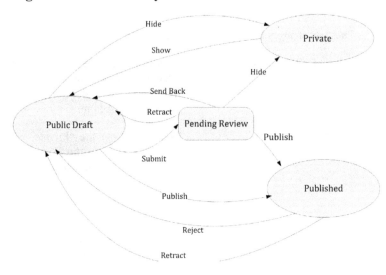

The following states are possible:

Public Draft

(green) Beginning state; newly added items are handled as public drafts. That means that any visitor to the website can view the items in this state. They will appear among the navigational elements and can be found by conducting a search. A public draft, however, can only be edited by its owner or by an editor.

Private

(red) In this state, an item is only visible to its owner or the Admin.

Pending Review

(orange) At item in this state has been submitted for review so that a reviewer can either publish or retract it. Both owners and reviewers can view the item, but only reviewers can make changes to it while in this state.

Published

(blue) Items in this state are accessible to all users. They can no longer be reworked by their owners or editors but only by Admins.

The applicable state changes are as follows:

Make Private

Transition from "Public draft" into the "Private state." The owner keeps an item from the public view, in order to continue working on it in private, for example.

Promote to Draft	Transition from the "Private" state into the "Public draft" state. With this step, the owner makes the private item available to the public.
Submit for publication	Transition from the "Private" state into the "Pending Review" state. The transition can be initiated by either the item's owner, an editor or the Admin.
Publish	Although items are already visible to visitors as drafts, it is still a good idea to publish them. Depending on how your website is configured, items might not be included among navigational elements until after they have been published.
Send Back	Transition from the "Pending review" state into the "Public draft" state. The reviewer thus rejects publication for an item.
Retract	Transition from the "Published" state or "Pending review" state into the "Public draft" state. The owner withdraws the item from public view.

Intranet/Extranet Workflow

The "Intranet/Extranet Workflow" is intended for websites which should either partly or completely be accessed only by a closed group of users. The primary difference from the community workflow lies in the ability to publish items externally as well as internally.

Figure A.3. Title

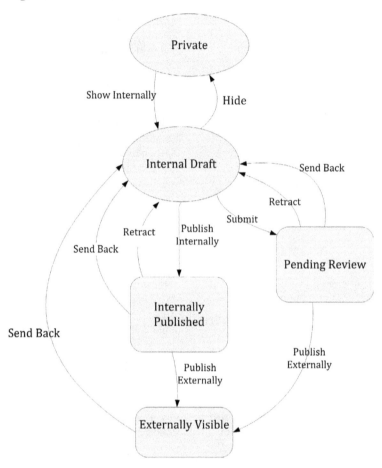

The following states are available:

Internal Draft

*(green)*Beginning state; newly added items are visible to all logged in users. Anonymous visitors to the website will have no access.

Private

(red) Beginning state; newly added items are automatically given the "private" state. A private item can only be viewed and edited by its owner or by an Admin.

Pending Review

(orange) An item in this state has been submitted for review so that a reviewer can either publish

or retract it. Both owners and reviewers can view the item, but only reviewers can make changes to the item while in this state.

Internally Published

(blue) Items with this state are accessible to all logged in users. They can no longer be edited by their owners or reviewers but only by Admins. Furthermore, internally published items are presented in prominent places on the website.

Externally visible

(blue) An item in this state is accessible to all who visit the website but can only be edited by Admins.

The respective state changes are as follows:

Make private

Transition from the "Internal draft" state into the "Private" state. This may be used when the owner decides to keep an item hidden from public view in order to work on it at leisure, for example.

Show internally

Transition from the "Private" state into the "Internal draft" state. With this step, the owner makes the item accessible to all logged in visitors.

Submit for publication

Transition from the "Private" state into the "Pending Review" state. The transition can be initiated by either the owner of the item, an editor or the Admin.

Publish internally

Transition from the "Internal draft" or "Pending review" states into the "Internally published" state. A reviewer makes the item accessible to registered users.

Publish externally

Transition from the "Pending review" or "Internally published" states into the "Externally visible" state. A reviewer makes the item accessible to both registered users and anonymous visitors to the website.

Send Back

Transition from the "Pending review" or "Internally published" states into the "Internal draft" state. A reviewer rejects an item for publication.

Retract

Transition from the "Pending review," "Internally published" or "Externally visible" states into the "Internal draft" state. The owner retracts the item from public view.

Appendix B. Administrator

Functions both Site Administrators & Managers Can Perform	Functions which only Managers Can Perform

Site Setup menu options:
- Calendar Settings
- Content Rules
- Editing
- HTML Filtering
- Image Handling
- Language
- Mail
- Markup
- Navigation
- Search
- Security
- Site
- TinyMCE Settings
- Types
- Users and Groups

Global Functions
- Add/Edit Collections
- Add/Edit Portlets
- Change Workflows on content items
- Edit/Delete any content
- View permissions on folders and items
- Cloning content by different users and moving it into another part of the site
- Able to access the Moderate Comments menu

Site Setup menu options
- Add Ons (activate, deactivate)
- Configuration Registry
- Dexterity content types
- Discussion
- Errors
- Maintenance (requires ZMI Access)
- Syndication
- Theming
- Zope Management Interface

Also: has access to any Add-On menus.

Index

www.ingramcontent.com/pod-product-compliance
Lightning Source LLC
Chambersburg PA
CBHW071420050326
40689CB00010B/1914